To the Student

This book contains exciting articles for you to read and enjoy. They tell about real-life adventures, unusual animals, famous people, interesting places, and important events.

There are questions after each article to help you think about and remember what you have read. The last question will give you a chance to write about the topic of the article.

Comprehension means "understanding." Good readers comprehend what they read. You can become a better reader and writer as you go through this book and focus on understanding.

Continental Press
Elizabethtown, PA 17022

Credits

Editorial Development: Matt Baker, Beth Spencer

Editorial Support: Joyce Ober, Anthony Moore

Cover and Interior Design: Joan Herring

Illustrators: Pages 14, 15; 64, 65; 76, 77 Margaret Lindmark
Pages 24, 25; 84, 85; 88, 89; 94, 95 Rob Williams

Photo Credits: Front cover: *Bald eagle, saguaro cactus, giraffes:* www.photos.com; *clownfish:* www.istockphoto.com/redtwiggy; *Mt. Rushmore:* www.istockphoto.com/megasquib; *open book:* www.istockphoto.com/mstay; Pages 4, 5: Library of Congress Prints and Photographs Division, LC-USZ62-59431; Pages 6, 7: www.istockphoto.com/davidp; Pages 8, 9: Library of Congress Prints and Photographs Division, LC-USZ62-98066; Pages 10, 11: NASA/JPL-Caltech; Pages 12, 13: www.wikipedia.org; Pages 18, 19: Getty Images; Pages 20, 21: www.istockphoto.com/tibet6688; Pages 22, 23: www.istockphoto.com/pomortzeff; Pages 26, 27: www.istockphoto.com/lissart; Pages 28, 29: Library of Congress Prints and Photographs Division, LC-USZ62-60139; Pages 30, 31: www.istockphoto.com/Tommounsey; Pages 32, 33: www.wikipedia.org; Pages 34, 35: Getty Images; Pages 36, 37: www.istockphoto.com/cyrop; Pages 38, 39: www.photos.com; Pages 40, 41: www.istockphoto.com; Pages 42, 43: www.photos.com; Pages 44, 45: Library of Congress Prints and Photographs Division, LC-USZ62-7816; Pages 46, 47: NASA-LaRC; Pages 50, 51: www.istockphoto.com/PaulWolf; Pages 52, 53: www.istockphoto.com/johnsfon; Pages 54, 55: www.wikipedia.org; Pages 56, 57: Library of Congress Prints and Photographs Division, LC-DIG-ggbain-12209; Pages 58, 59: www.photos.com; Pages 60, 61: AP/Wide World Photos; Pages 62, 63: www.istockphoto.com; Pages 66, 67: www.istockphoto.com/aleksander; Pages 68, 69: AP/Wide World Photos; Pages 70, 71: www.wikipedia.org; Pages 74, 75: www.photos.com; Pages 78, 79: www.wikipedia.org; Pages 80, 81: www.wikipedia.org; Pages 82, 83: www.photos.com; Pages 86, 87: www.photos.com; Pages 90, 91: NOAA Collection; Pages 92, 93: www.photos.com

ISBN 978-0-8454-1684-6

Contents

How does a person become president of the United States?

1 The president of the United States has one of the most powerful and important jobs in the world. Getting the job isn't easy. Fewer than 50 people have held it. In order to become president, you must meet some basic qualifications. Then you must win the election.

2 There are three basic requirements for becoming the president. The U.S. Constitution says that a presidential candidate must be at least 35 years old, be a natural-born citizen of the United States, and have lived in the United States for at least 14 years. But that's just the beginning. The election process has four parts.

3 The first part of the election is the primaries and caucuses. In these local elections, members of each political party get to vote on the person they want to represent them in the general election.

4 After the primaries and caucuses, each political party holds a national convention. At these exciting gatherings, each party chooses the person they want to run for president. The person they nominate then selects a running mate. The running mate is the person the nominee wants as his or her vice president.

5 In November of an election year, the general election is held. People in each state vote for the person they want to become president. But getting the most individual votes doesn't mean you've won the election. You have to win the electoral college to become president.

6 The candidate who gets the most votes in a state gets that state's electoral votes. The number of electoral votes a state has depends on the number of people who live there. A candidate must get 270 electoral votes to become president of the United States.

Circle the correct answer for questions 1–5.
Write your answer to question 6 on a separate piece of paper.

1. Each party nominates the person they want to run for president at the ______.
   A primary
   B electoral college
   C general election
   D national convention

2. Which word in paragraph 2 means "a person who wants to be elected to office"?
   A citizen
   B election
   C candidate
   D president

3. What happens before the national convention?
   A The president is elected.
   B The general election is held.
   C Primaries and caucuses are held.
   D People attend the electoral college.

4. The article is mostly about ______.
   A the election process
   B the national convention
   C how to become a citizen
   D the qualities of a good president

5. You can decide from the article that a person who is not a citizen of the United States ______.
   A cannot become president
   B would be the best choice for president
   C can choose a running mate who is a citizen
   D has to win the general election to become president

6. In order to get elected, a candidate for president of the United States has to convince people to vote for him or her. Write a speech to convince your classmates to elect you as class president.

How do animals hide in plain sight?

1 In order to survive, most animals need a way to hide themselves from predators and prey. To conceal themselves, many animals use camouflage to blend in with their environment.

2 The most basic kind of camouflage is blending. Blending is when an animal's coloring generally matches its surroundings. Polar bears, grasshoppers, tree frogs, and lizards are all examples of animals that have coloring that matches their environment. The arctic fox even changes its coat twice a year. It has a white coat in the winter to match the snow. In the summer, it has a brown coat to blend in with the trees and the grass.

3 Other animals have patterns, or special markings, that make the outlines of their body harder to see. These patterns are specially suited to the animal's environment. For example, an animal that lives in long grass may have long vertical stripes. A zebra's stripes seem to run off its edges. This makes the outline of its body hard to see. To a lion, it is almost impossible to tell one zebra from the whole herd.

4 Some animals camouflage themselves by using a special combination of shape, color, and movement to look like something else in their environment. The walking stick's shape, color, and slow movement make it seem just like a twig on a tree.

5 Animals that do not have a special camouflage may use materials from their surroundings to blend in. Many animals use everything from rocks and leaves to bird droppings to hide themselves from their enemies. As animal species change, they are constantly developing new ways to protect themselves from danger.

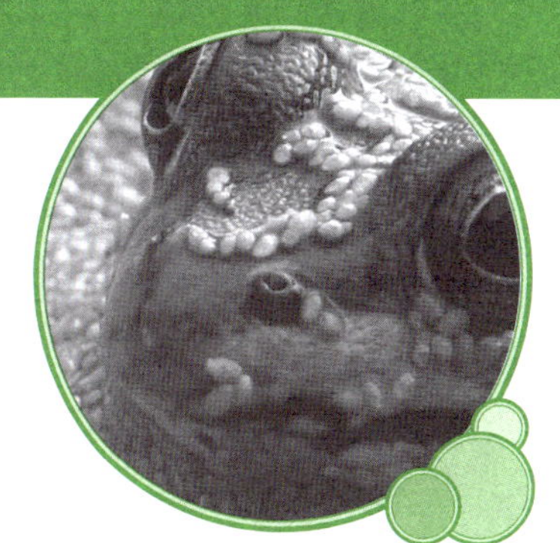

Circle the correct answer for questions 1–5.
Write your answer to question 6 on a separate piece of paper.

1. Animals use camouflage to ______.
   - **A** stand out
   - **B** blend in
   - **C** find food
   - **D** attract mates

2. Which word in paragraph 1 means "hide"?
   - **A** survive
   - **B** conceal
   - **C** camouflage
   - **D** environment

3. A zebra's stripes make ______.
   - **A** its outline hard to see
   - **B** it blend in with trees
   - **C** it look like another animal
   - **D** it easier for lions to see them

4. The article is mostly about ______.
   - **A** the life of a walking stick
   - **B** a zebra's special markings
   - **C** the ways animals camouflage themselves
   - **D** the way the arctic fox's coat changes color

5. *Match* can have the following meanings. Mark the meaning used in paragraph 2.
   - **A** a competition
   - **B** to blend with
   - **C** to fit together
   - **D** a stick for lighting fires

6. Think about an animal, such as a chameleon, that uses camouflage. Write a description of the animal. Tell how its appearance helps it blend in with its surroundings.

Who was the Wizard of Menlo Park?

1 Thomas Alva Edison was born in Ohio in 1847. As a child, he was curious about the world around him. His mother taught him reading, writing, and arithmetic. He also taught himself by reading about things that interested him and conducting experiments. He only attended school for a few months.

2 When Edison was young, electricity was still new. People never dreamed that it would one day light entire cities. Thomas Edison changed that. Working in his laboratory in Menlo Park, New Jersey, Edison invented the first successful electric light bulb. In December 1879, he demonstrated his lighting system by lighting the Menlo Park laboratory. Later, he helped bring in the electric age by setting up the first electrical power distribution company.

3 Edison also made important contributions to the music, motion picture, and telephone industries. He invented the first phonograph. This was the first machine that could record and reproduce sound. He also created a kinetoscope for viewing films, and he improved on Alexander Graham Bell's telephone design.

4 Thomas Edison believed in the importance of hard work. He often worked 20 hours a day. He is quoted as saying "Genius is 1 percent inspiration and 99 percent perspiration." By the time of his death at age 84, he had patented 1,093 inventions and earned the nickname "The Wizard of Menlo Park."

Circle the correct answer for questions 1–5.
Write your answer to question 6 on a separate piece of paper.

1. Thomas Edison helped bring in the electric age by ______.
   - **A** creating a kinetoscope
   - **B** improving the telephone
   - **C** inventing a machine that could record sound
   - **D** setting up the first electrical power distribution company

2. Which word in paragraph 2 means "showed how something works"?
   - **A** demonstrated
   - **B** dreamed
   - **C** changed
   - **D** helped

3. Which paragraph explains how Thomas Edison felt about hard work?
   - **A** 1
   - **B** 2
   - **C** 3
   - **D** 4

4. Thomas Edison lit up his laboratory to ______.
   - **A** show how his lighting system worked
   - **B** show how the kinetoscope worked
   - **C** conduct experiments
   - **D** play his phonograph

5. Thomas Edison earned his nickname because ______.
   - **A** he only attended school for a few months
   - **B** he patented 1,093 inventions
   - **C** he worked 20 hours a day
   - **D** he lived for 84 years

6. Compare the inventions of electric light and the telephone. Which is more important? Why?

What is it like on Venus?

1 No one has ever set foot on the planet Venus, but humans have a pretty good idea of what it looks like. That is because on May 4, 1989, the United States sent a special space probe, *Magellan,* to explore that planet. This spacecraft took pictures of Venus's surface. And the images it sent back were amazing.

2 Venus is about the same size as Earth, but it is closer to the sun. It is also much hotter and drier than Earth. In fact, over 80% of Venus is covered by rocks that were formed a half billion years ago by volcanoes. And there is no water at all on the planet's surface. Venus has no plants or animals, either. In fact, there are no signs of life on Venus.

3 *Magellan* sent back pictures of the tens of thousands of volcanoes that can be seen from space. As far as scientists can tell, none of them are still active, unlike some volcanoes on Earth. But hundreds of them are huge, nevertheless. Some of Venus's volcanoes are more than 150 miles in diameter. That's about the size of the state of Maine!

4 Will people ever get a closer look at Venus? Perhaps someday humans will travel there, just as they have gone to the moon. But for now the pictures from *Magellan* tell about Earth's solar system neighbor. And these photos will be teaching scientists about Venus for years to come.

Circle the correct answer for questions 1–5.
Write your answer to question 6 on a separate piece of paper.

1. Venus is ______ than Earth.
   A farther from Mercury
   B farther from the sun
   C hotter and drier
   D much larger

2. Which word in paragraph 1 means "vehicle sent into space to collect information"?
   A idea
   B probe
   C planet
   D surface

3. Which paragraph tells about the size of the volcanoes on Venus?
   A 1
   B 2
   C 3
   D 4

4. Animals cannot survive on Venus mainly because ______.
   A the planet has no plants or water
   B the planet has a rocky surface
   C the planet has huge volcanoes
   D the planet is hot and dry

5. You can decide from the article that a space probe was used to explore Venus's surface because ______.
   A the heat is too intense for astronauts
   B it can take better pictures than astronauts
   C it is less expensive than sending astronauts
   D the volcanoes are too dangerous for astronauts

6. Imagine that you are part of the first team of astronauts to explore Venus. Write a journal entry that describes the experience. What are you wearing? What do you see and feel?

What was the *Hindenburg?*

1 At one time, ships sailed in the air. These airships, similar to blimps today, were like giant balloons. They could float in the air because they were filled with hydrogen. Hydrogen is a gas that is lighter than air but burns easily. One of the largest airships was the 804-foot *Hindenburg.* It was also one of the last.

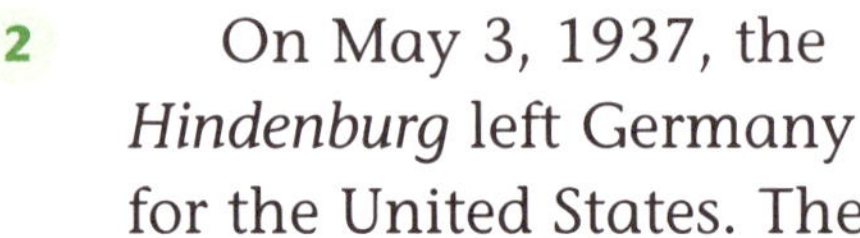

2 On May 3, 1937, the *Hindenburg* left Germany for the United States. The journey across the Atlantic was rainy but pleasant, and by late afternoon on May 6, the giant airship was over its landing field in New Jersey. Because of a thunderstorm, the *Hindenburg* couldn't start coming down until about 7:20 that evening. Then landing lines were thrown to the ground crew. The 200 men began pulling the huge ship down.

3 At 7:25, there was a popping sound. A small flash of flame appeared in the tail of the *Hindenburg.* Moments later, a second explosion was heard. A huge ball of fire shot toward the nose of the ship. As the flaming airship crashed, the ground crew dashed into the fiery wreck. Bravely, they tried to pull the passengers to safety.

4 Within seconds, the fire had turned the *Hindenburg* into a heap of twisted metal. In all, 36 lives were lost. After the disaster, travel by airship was no longer thought to be safe. The day of the giant passenger airships was over.

Circle the correct answer for questions 1–5.
Write your answer to question 6 on a separate piece of paper.

1. Airships could float through the air because of ______.
   - **A** balloons
   - **B** oxygen
   - **C** hydrogen
   - **D** rain

2. Which word in paragraph 4 means "a terrible happening"?
   - **A** metal
   - **B** travel
   - **C** disaster
   - **D** passenger

3. Which paragraph tells how fast the *Hindenburg* burned?
   - **A** 1
   - **B** 2
   - **C** 3
   - **D** 4

4. What happened last in the article?
   - **A** The *Hindenburg* left Germany.
   - **B** The *Hindenburg* crashed to the ground.
   - **C** A flame appeared in the tail of the *Hindenburg*.
   - **D** The ground crew tried to pull passengers to safety.

5. *Lines* can have the following meanings. Mark the meaning used in paragraph 2.
   - **A** rows of people or things
   - **B** words spoken in a play
   - **C** long, thin marks
   - **D** ropes or wires

6. Even though the *Hindenburg* disaster happened in real life, its journey sounds like the plot of a disaster movie. Write a paragraph that summarizes the plot of a disaster movie that you would like to see made.

What is color blindness?

1 The human eye is like a living movie camera. It can adjust to light, distance, and many other conditions. When people's eyes cannot do a perfect job, they have to wear glasses. But there is one problem that even glasses are not able to correct. That problem is color blindness.

2 Color blindness is not really the right word to use. Most "color-blind" people can see some colors. So color confusion would be a better description. The official name for this difficulty is Daltonism. The name comes from John Dalton, who was the first to study the problem.

3 There are at least three different kinds of color confusion. Confusing yellow and blue is one type of Daltonism. It is often caused by illness. Two other kinds of color confusion are more common. Both types confuse red and green. But in one kind, the person can see different shades of red. In the other, the person can see shades of green. These two types of Daltonism are thought to be inherited. They seem to be handed on by the mother, even if she has no trouble with colors herself.

4 Most people with Daltonism get along just as well as people without it. When a traffic light changes from red to green, for example, they can tell the difference in how bright the light is. They may not even know that their world of color is different. All people have their own world of color, and nobody knows exactly what someone else sees.

Circle the correct answer for questions 1–5.
Write your answer to question 6 on a separate piece of paper.

1. Daltonism is another name for ______.
   - **A** a shade of red
   - **B** a camera
   - **C** John Dalton
   - **D** color confusion

2. Which word in paragraph 3 means "got from older family members"?
   - **A** caused
   - **B** inherited
   - **C** handed
   - **D** thought

3. Which paragraph tells how the human eye works?
   - **A** 1
   - **B** 2
   - **C** 3
   - **D** 4

4. The Daltonism that confuses yellow and blue is often caused by ______.
   - **A** sun exposure
   - **B** eye injury
   - **C** genetics
   - **D** illness

5. You can conclude from the article that ______.
   - **A** traffic lights should be white
   - **B** there are many shades of blue
   - **C** people with Daltonism can't see purple
   - **D** people may not know a friend has Daltonism

6. Imagine that you have a form of Daltonism. Write about how your life would be different from a person with normal vision. What would be particularly difficult?

When did women first vote?

1 On a sunny Tuesday in November 1920, the United States first allowed women to vote. That day nearly eight million women voters helped elect a new president.

2 Women's right to vote is certainly accepted now. But when women first wanted to vote, most people laughed at the idea. They said women belonged at home. One U.S. president even said, "Sensible women do not want to vote."

3 Women first began to organize for the right to vote in 1848. This was at a women's rights meeting in Seneca Falls, New York. Some women stated it was their duty to vote. Since they paid taxes just as men did, they believed they should vote. Didn't Americans fight and win the Revolution so they could have a voice in government? Women felt the same way those early Americans did.

4 Over the next 70 years, women spoke out in public, wrote letters, and marched. They were called "suffragettes" because they were seeking suffrage, or the right to vote. Slowly, more and more men agreed that women must have the same rights they did. Many states had passed laws of their own to give women the right to vote. In Wyoming, women had voted since 1869. Finally, in 1919, the United States passed the Nineteenth Amendment to the Constitution. It gave all American women the right to vote. A year later, they voted in their first presidential election. Now, women themselves are voted into office.

Circle the correct answer for questions 1–5.
Write your answer to question 6 on a separate piece of paper.

1. In 1920, women voters helped elect a ______.
   - **A** government
   - **B** president
   - **C** woman
   - **D** king

2. Which word in paragraph 4 means "a contest for public office"?
   - **A** right
   - **B** election
   - **C** suffrage
   - **D** Amendment

3. Which paragraph tells when women first organized for the right to vote?
   - **A** 1
   - **B** 2
   - **C** 3
   - **D** 4

4. What happened first in history?
   - **A** Women began to vote in Wyoming.
   - **B** Women voted in a U.S. presidential election.
   - **C** Women began to organize for the right to vote.
   - **D** The United States passed the Nineteenth Amendment.

5. You can decide from the article that it was ______ to keep women from voting.
   - **A** unfair
   - **B** costly
   - **C** helpful
   - **D** necessary

6. Name a cause today that you believe in strongly and would be willing to work for. Describe your cause and try to persuade others to believe in it.

How do insects survive the winter?

1 Most insects go through all the stages of their life in one year. The stages are often timed to follow the changes of the seasons. In the summer, you will find insects everywhere. This is the time for mating and laying eggs. But by late fall, all the insects are gone from places where winter will be cold. Some of them die, and some go into their winter stage.

2 Insects that die in the fall have already laid their eggs. Their young will come out in the spring. Tiny aphid eggs spend the winter hidden in dead grasses. Katydid eggs are tucked on the leaves and twigs of certain trees. Other insects also have special hiding places. They all try to make sure their eggs will get through the winter safely.

3 Most caterpillars survive the winter in the pupa stage. This means the caterpillar makes a warm, waterproof case for its winter home. Some bury their cocoons underground, while others put theirs on twigs and branches. In the spring, each caterpillar comes out as a butterfly or moth.

4 There are other ways for insects to spend the winter, too. Monarch butterflies migrate. They fly hundreds of miles from the cold north to the warmer south. Ladybugs also survive as adults, gathering under rocks and fallen logs. Honeybees lower their numbers and seal off their hive. Then they live off their honey until spring. In the insect world, no way of surviving the winter is overlooked.

Circle the correct answer for questions 1–5.
Write your answer to question 6 on a separate piece of paper.

1. One insect that survives the winter as an adult is the ______.
   - **A** katydid
   - **B** caterpillar
   - **C** ladybug
   - **D** aphid

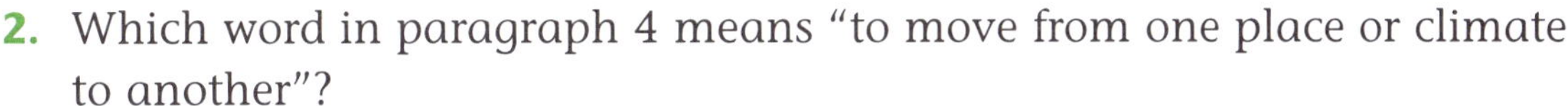

2. Which word in paragraph 4 means "to move from one place or climate to another"?
   - **A** survive
   - **B** migrate
   - **C** lower
   - **D** spend

3. Which paragraph tells what honeybees do in the winter?
   - **A** 1
   - **B** 2
   - **C** 3
   - **D** 4

4. You can decide from the article that insects are ______.
   - **A** likely to have long lives
   - **B** skilled at protecting their eggs
   - **C** not able to survive the winter
   - **D** exactly alike in how they deal with winter

5. *Seal* can have the following meanings. Mark the meaning used in paragraph 4.
   - **A** special design stamped into wax
   - **B** an animal of the sea
   - **C** small paper sticker
   - **D** close tightly

6. How are insects like birds in the winter? How are they different?

What is the Great Wall of China?

1 About 2,200 years ago, the emperor of China was worried. Raiders from the north were pouring through the mountains to attack his people. To keep his country safe, the emperor decided to build a wall.

2 The emperor put one of his generals in charge of an army of about one million workers. The huge army worked through the heat of summer and the cold of winter, year after year. They dug ditches for the base of the wall. They made bricks of clay or dirt. They piled stone upon stone. Thousands of workers died and may have been buried in the wall. After seven years, much of the wall was completed, but later emperors added to it. The latest addition was made less than 400 years ago.

3 The Great Wall looks like a giant brick snake. Stretching for more than 1,500 miles, it could reach from Boston to New Orleans. The base of the wall is 15 to 30 feet wide, and 8 soldiers can march side by side along its top. In most places, the wall is 24 feet tall. Every few hundred yards, however, is a 40-foot-high watchtower. There are 25,000 of them in all.

4 Parts of the Great Wall of China are still standing. In a way, the wall is now a bridge to the past. The world's longest wall helps us understand the history of one of the world's oldest countries.

Circle the correct answer for questions 1–5.
Write your answer to question 6 on a separate piece of paper.

1. The Great Wall of China was started about ______ years ago.
   - **A** 2,200
   - **B** 1,500
   - **C** 400
   - **D** 30

2. Which word in paragraph 2 means "long, narrow areas hollowed out of the ground"?
   - **A** ditches
   - **B** generals
   - **C** emperors
   - **D** bricks

3. Which paragraph tells how many people worked on the wall?
   - **A** 1
   - **B** 2
   - **C** 3
   - **D** 4

4. What led to the building of the Great Wall of China?
   - **A** The army was looking for work.
   - **B** Raiders were on their way to attack.
   - **C** There were several tons of stone available.
   - **D** The emperor wanted to impress other countries.

5. *Safe* can have the following meanings. Mark the meaning used in paragraph 1.
   - **A** a metal box to hold valuables
   - **B** not out on the bases
   - **C** free from danger
   - **D** cautious

6. What does building the Great Wall tell you about China and the Chinese people?

What is the largest flower in the world?

1 The world's largest flower is the rafflesia, or flower lotus. It is 36 inches wide and weighs 15 pounds. Some rafflesia grow to 42 inches, as tall as a 5-year-old child.

2 This huge flower is very rare. It only grows in rain forests on the islands of Sumatra and Borneo. The flower lotus has no roots or green leaves. It is a parasite (PAR•uh•syt), a plant that lives off another plant.

3 The flower lotus needs wild grapevines in order to live. Squirrels and other animals chew on grapevines for food, which cuts open the vine. Insects carry the sticky flower lotus seeds on their bodies. When the insects land on an opened vine, the seeds stick to the plant. Soon, the vine grows a new covering over the seed. The growing seed becomes part of the grapevine, taking food from it. The grapevine doesn't seem to mind sharing with the flower lotus. A year and a half later, a flower lotus bud pushes through the surface of the vine. The bud is only two inches wide and looks like a tiny cabbage. The bud grows for nine more months before it blooms.

4 The flower lotus has five bright red leathery petals covered with raised yellow dots. Stiff spikes protect the seeds in the flower's center. This brilliant flower only lives for four days. Then the colorful petals curl up and turn black. In a few weeks, all that is left is a slimy black mass that looks and smells like a dead animal. The smell draws many flies and other insects, and they carry the seeds to another waiting grapevine. The cycle begins again.

Circle the correct answer for questions 1–5.
Write your answer to question 6 on a separate piece of paper.

1. The flower lotus does *not* have ______.
   - A buds
   - B seeds
   - C petals
   - D leaves

2. Which word in paragraph 4 means "something that is repeated regularly"?
   - A mass
   - B cycle
   - C smell
   - D spikes

3. Which paragraph tells about the size of the flower lotus?
   - A 1
   - B 2
   - C 3
   - D 4

4. What happens first in the life cycle of the flower lotus?
   - A The bud grows for nine months.
   - B Insects carry seeds to grapevines.
   - C The grapevine grows a covering over the seed.
   - D The bud pushes through the surface of the vine.

5. You can decide from the article that insects ______ the flower lotus.
   - A help
   - B harm
   - C avoid
   - D destroy

6. Describe another situation in which members of the plant and animal kingdoms help one another to survive.

What was the Pony Express?

1 When gold was discovered in California in 1848, many people began traveling west in hopes of striking it rich. At the time, the telegraph line only went as far as St. Joseph, Missouri. The only way to communicate with family and friends back east was by mail. However, it often took months for letters to arrive.

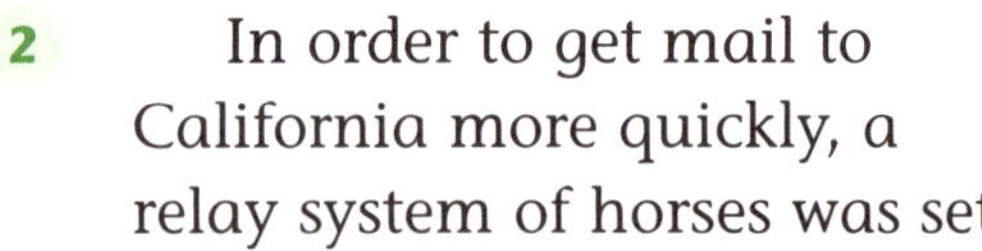

2 In order to get mail to California more quickly, a relay system of horses was set up. This relay team was called the Pony Express. The Pony Express set up stations about every 10 miles between St. Joseph, Missouri, and Sacramento, California. The Pony Express riders changed to a fresh horse at each station. A skilled rider could transfer himself and his mail pouch to a new horse in a single leap. Each rider rode for 75 to 100 miles. Their goal was to deliver the mail as quickly as possible.

3 The first Pony Express run began in St. Joseph on April 3, 1860 and ended in Sacramento on April 13. The fastest Pony Express delivery was in March 1861 when Abraham Lincoln became the president. His speech was delivered in 7 days and 17 hours.

4 Many people think that the Pony Express lasted for a long time. It was actually only in service for 16 months. When telegraph service became available across the United States, the Pony Express was no longer necessary. Although it lasted for a short time, the Pony Express remains an exciting chapter in American history.

Circle the correct answer for questions 1–5.
Write your answer to question 6 on a separate piece of paper.

1. The goal of the Pony Express was to ______.
   - **A** deliver mail quickly
   - **B** help people travel west
   - **C** help people strike it rich
   - **D** help establish a telegraph service

2. Which word in paragraph 4 means "needed"?
   - **A** exciting
   - **B** actually
   - **C** available
   - **D** necessary

3. Which paragraph explains the process of delivering mail by Pony Express?
   - **A** 1
   - **B** 2
   - **C** 3
   - **D** 4

4. The end of the Pony Express was caused by ______.
   - **A** telegraph service across the country
   - **B** people moving east instead of west
   - **C** the election of President Lincoln
   - **D** a lack of skilled riders

5. You can conclude from the article that a Pony Express rider had to be ______.
   - **A** kind and gentle
   - **B** quick and brave
   - **C** slow and cautious
   - **D** intelligent and funny

6. Imagine that you are writing an ad to hire riders for the Pony Express. Write an ad that would convince someone to take the job. Use persuasive words to make the position sound exciting.

How do birds migrate?

1 When animals migrate, they move from one part of the world to another. Many animals migrate. Birds are the most well-known seasonal travelers. During autumn, the shorter days and cooler nights cause many birds to begin their journey toward places where the temperatures are warmer and food is easier to find.

2 To prepare for the long journey, many birds molt. They shed their old, worn feathers and replace them with new ones. Then they eat and eat in order to build up enough fat for the long journey ahead. Many birds almost double their weight before they migrate.

3 One of the great mysteries of migration is how birds find their way. Birds that migrate during the daytime often use landmarks such as mountain ranges, rivers, and coastlines to find their winter homes. Other birds use the position of the sun to help them. Because water birds often migrate at night, they use the position of the stars to guide them. Some birds even seem to be able to use the Earth's magnetic field as a guide. Most birds use a combination of these techniques to guide them.

4 When winter is over, birds begin their journey home. People often wonder why birds do not stay in their southern homes all year. Many scientists believe that the longer days of the northern climates provide birds with more time each day to gather food and care for their young. And there is less competition from "local" birds for food. Whatever the reason, each spring the longer days and warmer temperatures bring birds back to their summer homes.

Circle the correct answer for questions 1–5.
Write your answer to question 6 on a separate piece of paper.

1. When winter is over, birds ______.
   - **A** stop gathering food
   - **B** walk instead of fly
   - **C** return to their summer homes
   - **D** journey toward warmer places

2. Which word in paragraph 2 means "shed"?
   - **A** molt
   - **B** prepare
   - **C** migrate
   - **D** double

3. Which paragraph tells how birds prepare for migration?
   - **A** 1
   - **B** 2
   - **C** 3
   - **D** 4

4. What is the main idea of the article?
   - **A** how birds molt
   - **B** how birds gather food
   - **C** how birds move to a different climate
   - **D** how birds gain weight for a long journey

5. *Spring* can have the following meanings. Mark the meaning used in paragraph 4.
   - **A** bounce
   - **B** a season
   - **C** a small body of water
   - **D** a coiled strip of metal

6. Write a one-paragraph summary of the article you just read.

Who was Thurgood Marshall?

1 Thurgood Marshall was born in 1908. Growing up, he saw that African Americans did not have the same rights as white people. At that time in America, blacks were not allowed to get an equal education, vote, or live where they wanted.

2 Determined to change things, Thurgood went to law school. He found that laws had been written to deny African Americans their rights. "These laws must be changed," Thurgood thought. One unjust law said black children and white children had to go to separate schools. The law said this was fair as long as the schools were equal. The "separate but equal" law also forced African Americans to live in different neighborhoods from whites and to use separate sections of theaters, restaurants, and public transportation.

3 Thurgood believed that "separate" was never "equal." In 1952, he presented a mountain of evidence to the Supreme Court, the highest court in the country. His evidence showed that the "separate but equal" law always meant "less than equal" for blacks. The judges thought about the case for more than a year. They finally agreed that Thurgood was right and changed the law. After that, African Americans had the right to go anywhere and do anything whites did.

4 In 1967, President Lyndon Johnson named Thurgood to the Supreme Court. He was the first African American to sit on the court. Today, African Americans do have equal rights. People like Thurgood Marshall made it happen.

Circle the correct answer for questions 1–5.
Write your answer to question 6 on a separate piece of paper.

1. Thurgood Marshall was named to the Supreme Court in ______.
   - **A** 1993
   - **B** 1967
   - **C** 1952
   - **D** 1908

2. Which word in paragraph 3 means "facts used to prove something"?
   - **A** mountain
   - **B** evidence
   - **C** judges
   - **D** court

3. Which paragraph tells when the "separate but equal" law was changed?
   - **A** 1
   - **B** 2
   - **C** 3
   - **D** 4

4. What happened last in the life of Thurgood Marshall?
   - **A** He went to law school.
   - **B** He was elected to Congress.
   - **C** He was named to the Supreme Court.
   - **D** He presented a case to the Supreme Court.

5. You can conclude from the article that laws are ______.
   - **A** always right
   - **B** never changed
   - **C** easy to change
   - **D** sometimes wrong

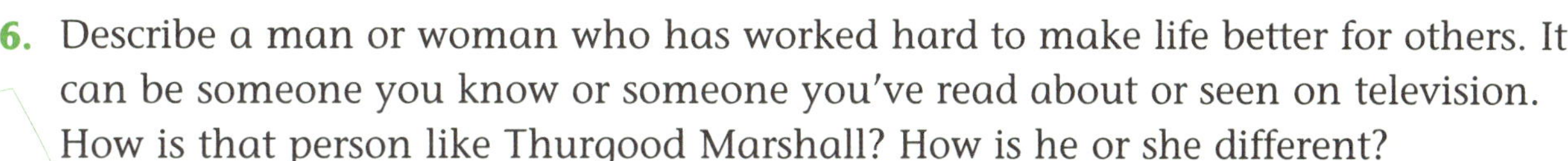

6. Describe a man or woman who has worked hard to make life better for others. It can be someone you know or someone you've read about or seen on television. How is that person like Thurgood Marshall? How is he or she different?

How do fingernails grow?

1 Our hard fingernails may seem quite different from the rest of the body's soft covering. But they are really just a special kind of skin. Like other parts of the body, our skin is made up of cells. The cells work together as a team even though they are not all alike. Some form the hair for our eyelashes and for our head. Others form fingernails.

2 Skin has two main layers. The thick inner layer is called the dermis. It is alive with nerves and blood vessels. The very thin outer layer is called the epidermis. It is made up of dead skin cells and has no nerves or blood vessels. These cells are constantly being rubbed off and replaced from below. And it is these cells that are used to form fingernails. Near the end of each finger, a special area called the matrix molds the dead epidermis cells together. Every day, the matrix adds new cells to the nail base, pushing the whole nail up toward the fingertip.

3 Because fingernails are dead skin, they don't hurt or bleed when you cut or tear them. The matrix, on the other hand, is part of the live layer of skin. And if it is hurt, it may not work right. It may grow twisted nails or no nails at all.

4 People don't often think about the growth going on at the ends of their fingers. Yet without nails our fingertips would not be as useful. Fingernails are a very special kind of skin indeed.

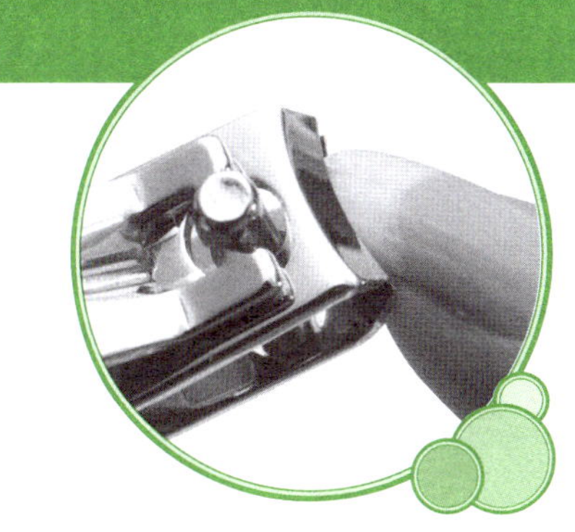

Circle the correct answer for questions 1–5.
Write your answer to question 6 on a separate piece of paper.

1. It does not hurt to cut a fingernail because the ______.
   - **A** cells are small
   - **B** nail grows longer
   - **C** nail has no nerves
   - **D** blood vessels are large

2. Which word in paragraph 2 means "always; continuously"?
   - **A** alive
   - **B** together
   - **C** pushing
   - **D** constantly

3. Which paragraph tells about the two layers of skin?
   - **A** 1
   - **B** 2
   - **C** 3
   - **D** 4

4. A twisted nail might mean that ______.
   - **A** the matrix was hurt
   - **B** a blood vessel was broken
   - **C** the nail should be removed
   - **D** the epidermis was rubbed off

5. You can conclude from the article that the matrix ______.
   - **A** is twisted
   - **B** shapes the nail
   - **C** cannot be hurt
   - **D** can cause hangnails

6. How are our fingernails like the claws on a cat or dog? How are they different?

Who made the first chewing gum?

1 Chewing gum was first used over a thousand years ago by the Mayas. The Mayas were a brilliant people who lived in Central America. They had a math system, a writing system—and chewing gum.

2 A tall tree with delicious fruit grew in the rain forests around the Mayan cities. It was called the sapodilla tree. The Mayas prized the tree for its fruit and for its strong red wood. They also found that if they cut the bark of the tree, a white fluid dripped out. The fluid would harden into a gummy lump. Even though it didn't have much taste, it was pleasant to chew. The material was called chicle (CHI•kuhl). And even today it is the main ingredient in all chewing gums.

3 For hundreds of years, the Mayas had the chicle all to themselves. Then travelers carried it to other countries. People everywhere seemed to like chewing it just as much as the Mayas did. In the 1860s, an inventor in the United States had an idea. He thought that chicle would be even more popular if it had a better taste. So he added a sweet flavor and watched sales of chewing gum grow. Other people copied the idea. The chewing gum business was born.

4 Not everyone thinks that chewing gum was such a wonderful discovery. But those who chew it think that there is nothing better.

Circle the correct answer for questions 1–5.
Write your answer to question 6 on a separate piece of paper.

1. The article does *not* tell about the ______ of chicle.
   - **A** use
   - **B** discovery
   - **C** color
   - **D** cost

2. Which word in paragraph 2 means "liquid"?
   - **A** lump
   - **B** fluid
   - **C** material
   - **D** ingredient

3. Which paragraph tells where chewing gum was first used?
   - **A** 1
   - **B** 2
   - **C** 3
   - **D** 4

4. The chewing gum business was born when ______.
   - **A** people got tired of chicle
   - **B** an inventor added a sweet flavor
   - **C** a new main ingredient was found
   - **D** chicle was taken around the world

5. *Brilliant* can have the following meanings. Mark the meaning used in paragraph 1.
   - **A** full of light
   - **B** magnificent
   - **C** very smart and clever
   - **D** a gem cut in a special way

6. Imagine that you have never chewed gum before and someone gives you a piece to try. What does it taste like? Do you like it? Why or why not?

What is REM sleep?

1 Do you know why you sleep? You may think it's because you're tired. Or perhaps you've been told sleep is good for you. Yet no one knows exactly why or how people sleep.

2 Until the early 1950s, most scientists thought the body and brain rested during sleep. Then a curious scientist watched people sleep. He noticed that during periods of between 5 and 30 minutes each, sleepers' eyes made rapid movements, as if they were watching something. He called these periods REM sleep, for Rapid Eye Movement. Periods when sleepers' eyes did not move he called non-REM sleep.

3 Whenever the scientist woke people during REM sleep, they were having vivid dreams. Measurements showed that sleepers' pulses went up quickly during REM sleep. Their breathing, heartbeat, and the blood going to the brain also increased. Far from being a time of rest, REM sleep is a time when the body is hard at work. Scientists still don't know the reason for this. Some believe REM sleep makes learning easier. Babies spend a lot of time in REM sleep. Because of this, some scientists believe that REM sleep helps the brain grow. Others think REM sleep is a time for the brain to empty the day's garbage.

4 One thing all the scientists agree on is that sleep is necessary. Without enough sleep, people make mistakes. Most major car accidents happen during the early morning hours, when people are sleepiest.

Circle the correct answer for questions 1–5.
Write your answer to question 6 on a separate piece of paper.

1. During REM sleep, a person's breathing and heartbeat ______.
   - **A** stop
   - **B** increase
   - **C** decrease
   - **D** stay the same

2. Which word in paragraph 3 means "colorful and lively"?
   - **A** easier
   - **B** empty
   - **C** vivid
   - **D** quickly

3. Which paragraph tells what happens when people don't get enough sleep?
   - **A** 1
   - **B** 2
   - **C** 3
   - **D** 4

4. What is the main idea of the article?
   - **A** REM sleep helps the brain grow.
   - **B** REM sleep has been observed by scientists.
   - **C** REM sleep is a time to empty the day's garbage.
   - **D** REM sleep is an active time when the body is hard at work.

5. You can decide from the article that REM sleep ______.
   - **A** has a restful effect on people
   - **B** can be avoided with lots of sleep
   - **C** is something that all people experience
   - **D** is something that all scientists agree on

6. Now that you've learned about REM sleep, think of a time when you were woken up during this time of your sleep. Why do you think this was REM sleep? Were you dreaming? What was the dream about?

How do crash-test dummies save lives?

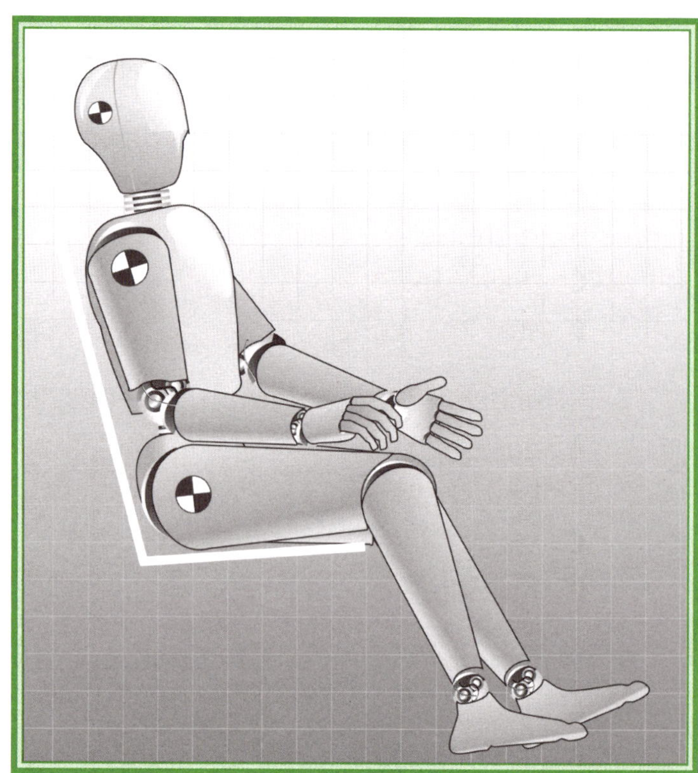

1 Each year, more than 40 thousand people are killed in car accidents in the United States. That's the bad news. The good news is that the number of deaths for each mile of travel is much lower than it used to be. Seat belts and government rules help save many lives. But for much of the improved safety, you can thank a bunch of dummies.

2 Carmakers crash cars into walls on purpose. Then they look for ways to make them safer. They also crash special "sleds" designed like the insides of cars. They have been using dummies in these tests since the 1950s.

3 Crash-test dummies are modeled on real human bodies. They are built in different sizes and weights to be like real men, women, and children. There are even "pregnant" dummies. Arms, legs, and heads are made in actual sizes. "Bones" and "joints" behave like real body parts. Wires work like nerves. Dummies wear clothes to show how a person slides around on the seat during an accident.

4 A crash-test dummy has a "tail" made of wires. It is connected to a computer. In a test, the computer measures more than 30 different items. The actual crash takes less than half a second. During that time, each item is measured 4,000 times.

5 Engineers often come up with new designs for crash-test dummies. They are looking for models that act just a little more like real human bodies. Then they can build cars that are even safer.

Circle the correct answer for questions 1–5.
Write your answer to question 6 on a separate piece of paper.

1. About how many people are killed in car crashes each year in the United States?
   - **A** 4,000
   - **B** 2,000
   - **C** 20,000
   - **D** 40,000

2. Which word in paragraph 3 means "parts of the body where two or more bones come together"?
   - **A** weights
   - **B** joints
   - **C** nerves
   - **D** dummies

3. Which paragraph tells how the dummies' reactions are measured?
   - **A** 1
   - **B** 3
   - **C** 4
   - **D** 5

4. Seat belts and government rules have led to ______.
   - **A** fewer drivers on the roads
   - **B** more money spent on gasoline
   - **C** fewer deaths for each mile of travel
   - **D** more car accidents in the United States

5. You can decide from the article that ______.
   - **A** crash-test dummies haven't changed since 1950
   - **B** crash-test dummies are a key factor in car safety
   - **C** engineers don't think crash-test dummies are important
   - **D** carmakers don't like to spend money on crash-test dummies

6. Pretend that a well-known carmaker (such as Chevrolet, Ford, Nissan, or Toyota) does not use crash-test dummies. Write a letter to persuade the company to use dummies to make its cars safer.

How do mountains form?

1 The Earth's surface is constantly changing. Sometimes the changes are caused by the movements of the plates that make up the Earth's crust. Other times, the changes are caused by dramatic events under the Earth's surface. Over time, even ordinary things like wind and rain can change the Earth's surface. These changes often result in the creation of landforms, such as mountains. There are five main kinds of mountains: fold mountains, dome mountains, block mountains, volcanic mountains, and plateau mountains.

2 Fold mountains form when the Earth's plates crash together. When this happens, layers of the crust are pushed up, forming mountains. The Himalayas were formed this way.

3 Dome mountains occur when magma pushes its way up under the Earth's surface. This melted rock forms a bulge that creates a mountain. The Black Hills of South Dakota are good examples of dome mountains.

4 Block mountains form when parts of the Earth's crust are forced up between cracks in a plate. The surface fractures and stacks, like blocks. The Sierra Nevada mountains were formed this way.

5 Volcanic mountains are formed from lava that cools and hardens after a volcano erupts. Over time, the cooled lava builds up to form a mountain. Mount St. Helens in Washington is an example of a volcanic mountain.

6 Plateau mountains are not formed as dramatically as the other kinds of mountains. Instead of being caused by sudden changes in the Earth, they are formed from plateaus that wind and rain have worn down over time.

Circle the correct answer for questions 1–5.
Write your answer to question 6 on a separate piece of paper.

1. Fold mountains form when ______.
   - **A** lava cools and hardens
   - **B** the Earth's plates crash together
   - **C** the Earth's crust is forced up between cracks
   - **D** magma pushes its way up under the Earth's surface

2. Which word in paragraph 3 means "melted rock"?
   - **A** mountain
   - **B** magma
   - **C** bulge
   - **D** dome

3. Which paragraph explains what happens when lava cools and hardens after a volcano erupts?
   - **A** 1
   - **B** 3
   - **C** 5
   - **D** 6

4. One effect of wind and rain is the creation of ______.
   - **A** volcanic mountains
   - **B** plateau mountains
   - **C** block mountains
   - **D** dome mountains

5. You can decide from the article that the mountains that form the most slowly are ______.
   - **A** volcanic mountains
   - **B** plateau mountains
   - **C** block mountains
   - **D** fold mountains

6. Some parts of the United States have mountains. Other parts have landforms such as deserts. Describe the landforms you can see in the part of the country where you live. What makes them unique?

What is the only continent that humans have never lived on?

1 Antarctica is the only continent that has never had a native population of humans. That's because its environment is so extreme that it's nearly impossible to live there for any length of time. It is one of the driest, highest, coldest, and windiest places on Earth.

2 Although Antarctica is covered in ice, it is actually the largest desert in the world. It gets just a little more rainfall than the Sahara desert. The dry conditions and freezing temperatures mean that very few living things can survive there. The lack of food and materials for building shelters has kept humans away for thousands of years.

3 The freezing temperatures in Antarctica naturally make it home to a lot of ice. The thickest sheet of ice in the world can be found in Antarctica. And 90% of the planet's ice exists in Antarctica.

4 In addition to the freezing temperatures and icy conditions, the sun rises and sets only twice a year at the South Pole. This means that there are six months of daylight in the summer followed by six months of darkness in the winter.

5 Advances in technology have made it easier for scientists to travel to Antarctica and survive in its harsh conditions. However, the constant darkness and bone-chilling temperatures of the winter months mean that even the rugged scientists who study Antarctica rarely stay longer than a few months at a time.

Circle the correct answer for questions 1–5.
Write your answer to question 6 on a separate piece of paper.

1. The only continent that has never had a native population of humans is ______.
   - A Africa
   - B Australia
   - C Antarctica
   - D North America

2. Which word in paragraph 5 means "continuous"?
   - A harsh
   - B rugged
   - C constant
   - D bone-chilling

3. Which paragraph explains why Antarctica is dark for part of the year?
   - A 1
   - B 2
   - C 3
   - D 4

4. People rarely stay longer than six months in Antarctica because ______.
   - A it is covered in ice
   - B it is too dark and cold
   - C there is very little rainfall
   - D they can't build a shelter there

5. You can decide from the article that ______.
   - A the best time to visit Antarctica is during the winter
   - B people will soon start living in Antarctica
   - C Antarctica is a difficult place to live
   - D it is easy to travel to Antarctica

6. Think of another place in the world that is difficult for humans to visit. How is it like Antarctica? How is it different?

How do olives get their taste?

1 Olives picked right from the tree have a nasty, bitter flavor. If you taste one, you'll want to spit it out. That's a very good idea. The bitter taste is made by a strong chemical that can upset your stomach.

2 No one knows how people learned that olives could be good to eat. Somehow they found that treating olives with lye and salt water changed their bitterness to a rich, pleasing flavor. This could be risky, though. The lye and salt probably poisoned more people than the bitter olives did.

3 The fresh olive's bitter taste comes from a burning chemical that is an acid. Lye, another burning chemical, is an alkali. When an acid and an alkali meet, they try to change each other. If they are equally strong, they form a new chemical that is neither acid nor alkali. This rule of chemistry is what makes olives taste good.

4 The olives are first soaked in a lye and water mixture. They must stay in the lye bath until the chemical seeps through to the hard pits in the center of the olives. It may take three days. An expert keeps testing the olives to find out if they are ready. This is not an easy or a safe job because of the burning lye. As soon as the olives have soaked up enough lye, they are taken out. The next step is to rinse them. This goes on for a week. Then a final soak in salt water brings out the safe, delicious olive taste most people know.

Circle the correct answer for questions 1–5.
Write your answer to question 6 on a separate piece of paper.

1. After a lye bath, olives are soaked in ______ to bring out their good flavor.
   - **A** acid
   - **B** alkali
   - **C** salt water
   - **D** wine vinegar

2. Which word in paragraph 2 means "dangerous"?
   - **A** rich
   - **B** pleasing
   - **C** bitter
   - **D** risky

3. Which paragraph tells how long the olives' lye bath may last?
   - **A** 1
   - **B** 2
   - **C** 3
   - **D** 4

4. What happens first after olives are picked?
   - **A** They are rinsed.
   - **B** They are tested.
   - **C** They are soaked in salt water.
   - **D** They are soaked in a lye and water mixture.

5. *Pits* can have the following meanings. Mark the meaning used in paragraph 4.
   - **A** the worst
   - **B** stones of a fruit
   - **C** holes in the ground
   - **D** sets one against the other

6. Write an article that explains all the steps needed to make a type of food.

Who led 300 slaves to freedom?

1 The young slave tied some scraps of food, a few coins, and a knife in a piece of cloth. With these supplies, Harriet Tubman planned to escape from her Maryland master. When darkness fell, Harriet dashed through the fields and into the woods. She headed toward Philadelphia where she knew she would be safe. To get there, Harriet had to travel on the "Underground Railroad."

2 It was 1849. Slavery was a way of life in some parts of the United States. The Underground Railroad had been set up to help slaves escape to the North. This railroad had no real trains. It did have "stations" and "conductors," though. Stations were places where slaves could rest during their journey to freedom. Conductors were the people who guided them.

3 With the help of several conductors, Harriet made her way to Philadelphia. There, a strange, wonderful feeling came over her. "I looked at my hands to see if I was the same person now that I was free," she said. "I felt like I was in heaven."

4 Harriet wanted others to share the wonderful feeling of freedom. She became a conductor on the Underground Railroad and returned to the South 19 times. Running through swamps and hiding in caves, she led more than 300 slaves to freedom. She was a daring conductor who never lost a single passenger.

Circle the correct answer for questions 1–5.
Write your answer to question 6 on a separate piece of paper.

1. The Underground Railroad had no ______.
   - **A** trains
   - **B** stations
   - **C** conductors
   - **D** passengers

2. Which word in paragraph 1 means "leftovers"?
   - **A** scraps
   - **B** coins
   - **C** supplies
   - **D** fields

3. Which paragraph tells how Harriet felt when she was free?
   - **A** 1
   - **B** 2
   - **C** 3
   - **D** 4

4. You can conclude from the article that Harriet Tubman was ______.
   - **A** a train conductor
   - **B** not physically active
   - **C** popular with slave owners
   - **D** a hero to African Americans

5. *Master* can have the following meanings. Mark the meaning used in paragraph 1.
   - **A** someone with power to rule and control
   - **B** a title for a young boy
   - **C** become very skilled in
   - **D** a teacher

6. Think about what it would be like to journey to freedom on the Underground Railroad. Write a short story that describes this experience.

Does sound travel on the moon?

1 Before any visitors reached the moon, astronomers described it as a silent place. They said that there could be no sounds at all there. Then astronauts landed on the moon and talked to one another as they explored its surface. Their voices were heard on Earth. Were the astronomers wrong?

2 To find the answer, we must know something about sound waves. Sound waves need solids, liquids, or gases to carry them along. On Earth, sounds travel through air to reach our ears. If there is no air, sound waves cannot travel. Imagine a television sealed in a glass case with all the air removed. You can see the power is turned on and the volume is turned up. Yet you will hear no sound because there is nothing to carry the sound waves.

3 The surface of the moon has no air either. So the astronomers were right. The moon is silent. Then how could the astronauts talk to each other while they were there? They went to the moon prepared. The astronauts carried equipment to send and receive radio waves. Radio waves are different from sound waves. They speed along at 186,000 miles per second. They do not need other material to carry them along. The astronauts could use radios to talk to each other and to people on Earth. But the moon itself was just as silent as ever.

Circle the correct answer for questions 1–5.
Write your answer to question 6 on a separate piece of paper.

1. There is no ______ on the moon.
   - **A** air
   - **B** dust
   - **C** space
   - **D** surface

2. Which word in paragraph 2 means "taken away"?
   - **A** removed
   - **B** sealed
   - **C** strike
   - **D** solids

3. The astronauts on the moon were able to talk to each other because ______.
   - **A** they used telephones
   - **B** they brought special equipment
   - **C** the surface of the moon has craters
   - **D** their voices were sent back to Earth

4. What is the main idea of the article?
   - **A** Radio waves travel on the moon, so astronauts used radios to communicate.
   - **B** Sound waves travel on the moon, so astronauts didn't need radios.
   - **C** Astronomers described the moon as a silent place.
   - **D** On Earth, sounds travel through the air.

5. You can conclude from the article that ______.
   - **A** you can't hear radio waves without the right equipment
   - **B** the astronauts were surprised that the moon was silent
   - **C** sound waves do not travel through water
   - **D** radio waves will not work inside a jar

6. Write a paragraph that explains what would make the moon a difficult place for a person to live.

What was the Trail of Tears?

1 For hundreds of years, the Cherokees had lived in the beautiful mountains and valleys of Georgia, Tennessee, and North Carolina. But then the United States became a nation and began to grow. White settlers came to the Native American lands. They saw the rich soil and well-run Cherokee farms. They also knew that gold had been found on Cherokee land. In 1830, the Cherokee Nation was ordered to move west. Land had been set aside for them in Indian Territory, now the state of Oklahoma.

2 Most of the Cherokees refused to move. "This is our home," they said. "We were here long before the white man came. This land is sacred to us. The spirits of our fathers rest here."

3 The Cherokees didn't fight the order with bows and arrows. They fought in the courts and in Congress. After eight long years, they won their case in the U.S. Supreme Court. But President Andrew Jackson refused to carry out the law. The Cherokees' cause was lost.

4 In the winter of 1838, the U.S. Army drove some 14,000 Cherokees from their homes. The 800-mile journey west took 6 months. Most of the Cherokees had to travel on foot. Hunger, cold, and sickness became their deadly enemies. Dozens of men, women, and children died and were buried along the trail. About 4,000 Cherokees never reached Oklahoma. And ever since, this long, sad march of the Cherokees has been known as the Trail of Tears.

Circle the correct answer for questions 1–5.
Write your answer to question 6 on a separate piece of paper.

1. The article does *not* tell about the ______ of the Cherokee Nation.
   - **A** farms
   - **B** schools
   - **C** court case
   - **D** long march

2. Which word in paragraph 4 means "a strong need or desire for food"?
   - **A** winter
   - **B** march
   - **C** hunger
   - **D** journey

3. Which paragraph tells why the Cherokees didn't want to move?
   - **A** 1
   - **B** 2
   - **C** 3
   - **D** 4

4. You can conclude from the article that ______.
   - **A** Native Americans were treated unfairly
   - **B** the U.S. Army was friendly to Native Americans
   - **C** Native Americans didn't mind moving to new land
   - **D** the U.S. government felt sorry for Native Americans

5. *Lost* can have the following meanings. Mark the meaning used in paragraph 3.
   - **A** gone
   - **B** missing
   - **C** not won
   - **D** unable to find the way

6. Write a letter to persuade President Jackson to carry out the law that said the Cherokees did not have to leave their land and move west.

Is the roadrunner a real bird?

1 The roadrunner is real. It lives in the deserts of the southwestern United States. You could mistake it for a very colorful chicken. The roadrunner's stringy brown feathers are tipped with white. Its long tail feathers shine with a greenish bronze. And its bright eyes are set in circles of blue and orange skin.

2 As its name says, the roadrunner loves to run by the side of the road. It even likes to race cars. It strides on long legs with its tail bobbing and its neck stretched out. For extra speed, the roadrunner uses its floppy wings to make long, gliding leaps. It is such a comical sight that a passing driver often slows down to watch. This gives the roadrunner its chance to dash ahead. When it has passed the car, the speedy bird is satisfied. It stops by tipping its tail over its back. Having "won" the race, it then swerves out of sight into the desert.

3 The roadrunner is also good at killing rattlesnakes. First it pokes the snake with its long, sharp beak. Each time the snake strikes back, the roadrunner jumps out of reach. At last the snake gets tired. The roadrunner leaps in for the kill, biting the snake at the back of the neck.

4 Because it is a good sport, a comic, and a snake killer, the roadrunner is very popular. It is especially admired by Native Americans. They call it the war bird or the snake bird. But their favorite name for the roadrunner is "crazy chicken."

Circle the correct answer for questions 1–5.
Write your answer to question 6 on a separate piece of paper.

1. The roadrunner is *not* ______.
   A a snake killer
   B a real bird
   C colorful
   D slow

2. Which word in paragraph 2 means "turns quickly and sharply"?
   A slows
   B leaps
   C strides
   D swerves

3. Which paragraph tells about the racing habits of the roadrunner?
   A 1
   B 2
   C 3
   D 4

4. You can decide from the article that the roadrunner ______.
   A wins most races with cars
   B looks like every other bird
   C has no problem catching food
   D is eaten by Native Americans

5. *Sport* can have the following meanings. Mark the meaning used in paragraph 4.
   A game that involves physical activity
   B one who is happy to win or lose
   C make fun of
   D boast

6. Describe the funniest animal you've ever seen.

Who were the cliff dwellers?

1 Across the southwestern United States are the ruins of ancient cities. Unlike most cities, these were built in huge caves high up in cliffs. How did the cities get there? Who built them?

2 For many hundreds—perhaps thousands—of years, Native Americans of the Southwest grew corn, beans, squash, and melons. They lived near their fields. Because there was a lot of rain then, crops grew well. Villages became larger as more people came to share the wealth.

3 Then tribes from farther north began raiding these peaceful people. To protect themselves, the villagers started to build their homes in caves at the top of nearby cliffs. They also dug holes called pit houses that were used for storage. The cliff dwellings were made of rock. Most buildings were two or three stories high with many small rooms. There were few doors on the ground level. The cliff dwellers used ladders to reach entrances on the roofs. In case of attack, the ladders could be pulled up. As many as 1,500 people could live in one of these cities.

4 Where did the cliff dwellers go? In about A.D. 1100, the rains stopped. Without enough water, the cliff dwellers probably moved farther south in search of better farmland. The soil had already been worn out by years of farming. In some places, it was just dust. Perhaps increasing enemy attacks also encouraged the cliff dwellers to leave. At one time people thought that the tribe became extinct. Now it is believed that they were in fact the ancestors of today's Pueblo people. So, while the cliff dwellings are empty, the people live on.

Circle the correct answer for questions 1–5.
Write your answer to question 6 on a separate piece of paper.

1. The article does *not* tell about the ______ of cliff dwellers.
   - **A** crops
   - **B** homes
   - **C** enemies
   - **D** animals

2. Which word in paragraph 3 means "houses"?
   - **A** entrances
   - **B** rooms
   - **C** dwellings
   - **D** stories

3. Which paragraph tells when the rains stopped?
   - **A** 1
   - **B** 2
   - **C** 3
   - **D** 4

4. What led the cliff dwellers to start building their homes in cliffs?
   - **A** Other tribes began raiding them.
   - **B** White settlers came to America.
   - **C** Villages became too large.
   - **D** The rains stopped.

5. *Ruins* can have the following meanings. Mark the meaning used in paragraph 1.
   - **A** damages
   - **B** economic collapse
   - **C** subject to frustration
   - **D** remains of something destroyed

6. Today these cliff dwellers, known as the Anasazi, remain a mystery. Give another theory for what might have happened to them and what makes you think so.

What is a manta ray?

1 The manta ray looks as if it comes from another world. But the manta ray and its ancestors have lived in our oceans for millions of years. Skin divers may catch a glimpse of a manta ray as it flaps through warm tropical seas like a giant bat. Sometimes it makes a powerful leap high into the air. Then it splashes down with a mighty bellyflop that can be heard all around.

2 The manta ray belongs to the shark family. Like its shark cousins, the manta ray is large and very strong. Its black body is shaped like a wide diamond with a long, thin tail. It is covered with a tough, leathery skin. When the manta ray swims, its sides move like a pair of huge wings. These sides are really special fins. They help the manta ray swim through the deep, blue water.

3 Many of the manta ray's shark cousins are fierce hunters. They mostly eat fish and other sea animals, but they will attack a human swimmer, too. The manta ray, on the other hand, just eats fish eggs, shrimp, small fish, and plants. It never bites people.

4 Even so, meeting a manta ray can be a bit frightening. Its flat body may be more than 20 feet wide and weigh about 3,000 pounds. It looks like a monster with its large open mouth, its staring eyes, and the two curved "horns" on top of its head. You can hardly blame people who called it the devilfish. But the manta ray doesn't deserve this name. It is a very gentle giant.

Circle the correct answer for questions 1–5.
Write your answer to question 6 on a separate piece of paper.

1. A manta ray belongs to the ______ family.
   - A bat
   - B bird
   - C shark
   - D shrimp

2. Which word in paragraph 4 means "earn; be worthy of"?
   - A deserve
   - B curved
   - C blame
   - D weigh

3. Which paragraph tells about the manta ray's food?
   - A 1
   - B 2
   - C 3
   - D 4

4. You can decide from the article that most swimmers ______ the manta ray.
   - A worship
   - B avoid
   - C feed
   - D pet

5. *Diamond* can have the following meanings. Mark the meaning used in paragraph 2.
   - A a playing card
   - B a baseball field
   - C a four-sided shape
   - D a sparkling, clear stone

6. Manta rays have been known to carry divers on their backs through the water. Imagine that you are a diver on the back of a manta ray. Describe your ride. Tell what you'd see and feel.

Who are The Ninety-Nines?

1 Amelia Earhart Drive runs past the airport in Oklahoma City. Here you will find the headquarters of The Ninety-Nines. In the building is a museum. It is full of exhibits from the early days of aviation. All the pilots in the pictures are women. The Ninety-Nines is the oldest female pilots' organization in the world.

2 The club began in 1929. Earlier that year, 20 women had taken part in a cross-country air race. One pilot was killed when her plane crashed. But 14 women finished the race.

3 The race built strong ties among the pilots. Some of them decided to start a club. They invited every licensed female pilot in the United States. There were 126 in all, and 99 joined. Amelia Earhart, America's most famous female pilot, became president of the club. It was her idea to name the club after the number of original members.

4 The Ninety-Nines today has more than 5,000 members around the world. The club puts on air races. It holds antique-plane rallies. It raises money for the training of young pilots. But its main goal is the same as it was in 1929—to have women taken seriously as fliers. The club backed Jerrie Cobb, who in 1959 almost became one of America's first astronauts. Perhaps The Ninety-Nines' proudest day came in 1973. That was when Bonnie Tiburzi became the first woman to pilot a plane for a major airline.

Circle the correct answer for questions 1–5.
Write your answer to question 6 on a separate piece of paper.

1. The Ninety-Nines is named for the ______.
   - **A** year the club was started
   - **B** number of original members in the club
   - **C** number of women who took part in an air race
   - **D** number of countries to which club members have flown

2. Which word in paragraph 1 means "the act of flying an airplane"?
   - **A** headquarters
   - **B** exhibits
   - **C** aviation
   - **D** airport

3. Which paragraph tells the main purpose of The Ninety-Nines?
   - **A** 1
   - **B** 2
   - **C** 3
   - **D** 4

4. What happened last in the history of The Ninety-Nines?
   - **A** A woman piloted a plane for a major airline.
   - **B** Amelia Earhart became club president.
   - **C** The club backed an astronaut.
   - **D** The club was formed.

5. *Ties* can have the following meanings. Mark the meaning used in paragraph 3.
   - **A** attaches
   - **B** a bond of affection
   - **C** cords used for fastening
   - **D** equal scores in contests

6. Why do you think it was hard for women to be accepted as pilots?

How was Crater Lake formed?

1 Mount Mazama is in what is now the state of Oregon. Once it was over 12,000 feet tall. Glaciers capped its top, and green trees spread across its lower slopes. The mountain seemed very peaceful.

2 But inside the volcano, a lot of things were happening. Pressure built up until the ground began to shake. Suddenly there was the deafening roar of an explosion. Hot stones shot up through Mount Mazama's peak. One terrible explosion followed another. Liquid rock boiled over the mountain's top. Hot streams of this lava rushed down the mountain into the valleys below. Scorching winds stirred up by the lava swept the trees from the slopes. Smoke, dust, and steam darkened the sky.

3 These days of fire and noise were followed by weeks of quiet. Then the explosions started again. So much lava poured out of the mountain that the inside of its peak became just a shell. Finally, thundering like hundreds of jets, Mazama's peak fell into the huge opening. In its place, a crater 6 miles wide and 4,000 feet deep faced the sky.

4 Slowly the mountain cooled. Little by little, rain and melting snow filled the crater to about 2,000 feet. In this way, the deepest lake in the United States was formed about 6,500 years ago. And the 20 square miles of blue water are today known as Crater Lake.

Circle the correct answer for questions 1–5.
Write your answer to question 6 on a separate piece of paper.

1. Crater Lake ______.
   - A was man-made
   - B is 2,000 years old
   - C is 12,000 feet deep
   - D was formed by a volcano

2. Which word in paragraph 2 means "very loud"?
   - A deafening
   - B terrible
   - C boiled
   - D liquid

3. Which paragraph tells how the crater filled with water?
   - A 1
   - B 2
   - C 3
   - D 4

4. What happened first when Crater Lake was formed?
   - A Mount Mazama's peak fell.
   - B Lava boiled over Mount Mazama's top.
   - C Pressure built up inside Mount Mazama.
   - D Scorching winds swept the trees from the slopes.

5. *Peak* can have the following meanings. Mark the meaning used in paragraphs 2 and 3.
   - A a pointed end
   - B the highest level
   - C reach the maximum
   - D the top of a mountain

6. Write a one-paragraph summary of the article you just read.

Who is Chinua Achebe?

1 When Chinua Achebe was a child in Africa, his mother and sister told him many strange and wonderful stories about his people, the Ibo of Nigeria. Chinua always liked hearing these tales from his family and other members of his tribe. He thought that someday he would like to be a storyteller, too.

2 At that time Chinua never dreamed that it was possible to make a living as a storyteller or writer. Once he started high school, Chinua began to read the great classics of Shakespeare, Dickens, and other British writers. He also read books about Africa and Africans that had been written by Europeans. He soon realized that these writers couldn't really understand life in Africa and what it was like to grow up African. He thought that the story of Africa should be told by an African. So Chinua decided to become the storyteller of his people.

3 Since then, Chinua Achebe has written many books. His first novel, *Things Fall Apart,* sold more than 2 million copies and was translated into 45 languages. Chinua also began a company in Nigeria to publish the works of other Africans. Much of his own writing, as well as what he publishes for others, is about the hard lives and problems of Africans in today's world.

4 In 1972, Chinua came to the United States to teach. Since then, he has traveled back and forth between Nigeria and the United States. He has won many awards for his work, but one honor was especially important. In 1986, the people of his village chose him as their town leader. In this way, they thanked Chinua Achebe for being their greatest storyteller.

Circle the correct answer for questions 1–5.
Write your answer to question 6 on a separate piece of paper.

1. Chinua Achebe is ______.
   - **A** a great actor
   - **B** a teacher and a writer
   - **C** a writer and a warrior
   - **D** the chief of the Ibo tribe

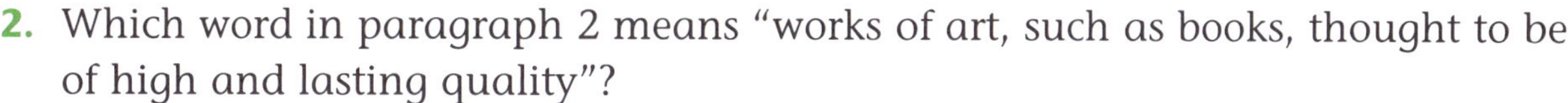

2. Which word in paragraph 2 means "works of art, such as books, thought to be of high and lasting quality"?
   - **A** writers
   - **B** Europeans
   - **C** classics
   - **D** Africans

3. Which paragraph tells about Chinua Achebe's publishing company?
   - **A** 1
   - **B** 2
   - **C** 3
   - **D** 4

4. What happened last in the life of Chinua Achebe?
   - **A** He read the great classics.
   - **B** His first book was published.
   - **C** He was chosen as town leader.
   - **D** He came to teach in the United States.

5. You can decide from the article that Chinua Achebe ______.
   - **A** is respected by Africans
   - **B** prefers teaching more than storytelling
   - **C** likes Nigeria better than the United States
   - **D** won't publish books by American authors

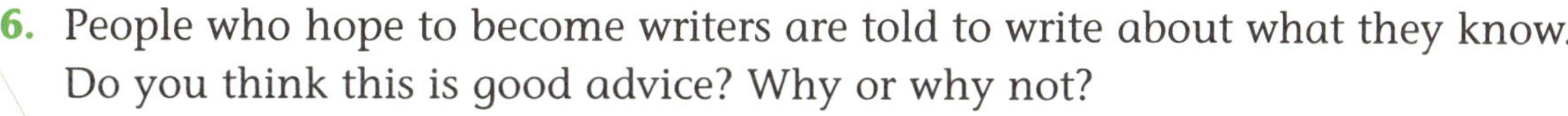

6. People who hope to become writers are told to write about what they know. Do you think this is good advice? Why or why not?

What are marsupials?

1 Australia is home to many of the world's strangest animals. There is the platypus, with its ducklike bill, its webbed feet, and its flat tail. There is also the noisy kookaburra, a small bird with a loud mouth. But many of Australia's most unusual creatures are marsupials.

2 Marsupials are a special kind of mammal. Their young are born after only two or three weeks and must finish developing outside their mother's body. Most marsupial babies do this in a cozy pouch on their mother's stomach. About a hundred million years ago, these animals were common all over the world. But in many places they could not stand up to stronger mammals and began to die off. Today, only a few kinds of opossum still live in North America. Most marsupials live in Australia. There and only there were they the main animal family.

3 Australian marsupials come in all sizes and shapes, from tiny pouched mice to the huge great gray kangaroo. There are about 170 different kinds in all. The Tasmanian devil looks like a cross between a cat and a monkey. The tree kangaroo looks like a cross between a kangaroo and a raccoon. Even the furry little koala looks more like a bear than what it is.

4 Maybe marsupials look so odd to Americans because they live so far away. But even in nature, these animals are unique. The island continent of Australia has been a safe place for marsupials to develop in their own special way.

Circle the correct answer for questions 1–5.
Write your answer to question 6 on a separate piece of paper.

1. Marsupials are all ______.
   A small
   B large
   C common
   D mammals

2. Which word in paragraph 4 means "being one of a kind; having no equal"?
   A odd
   B safe
   C special
   D unique

3. Which paragraph tells about some Australian animals that are not marsupials?
   A 1
   B 2
   C 3
   D 4

4. What led most marsupials outside Australia to die off?
   A hunting seasons
   B cold temperatures
   C stronger mammals
   D the Tasmanian devil

5. *Cross* has the following meanings. Mark the meaning used in paragraph 3.
   A meet in passing
   B marked by bad temper
   C an intersection of two lines
   D combination of characteristics

6. Koalas are shy little animals. Why do you think they are so popular all over the world?

What is bluegrass music?

1 Bluegrass started in Kentucky around 1938. It was started by Bill Monroe, a country musician. He played and sang the folk and religious music of the southern Appalachian Mountains. His instrument was the mandolin. He could "pick" its strings with lightning speed. Its high, clear sound seemed to match his soaring voice.

2 Radio made Bill Monroe a star. His "high, lonesome" sound traveled into hundreds of tiny communities in Kentucky, Tennessee, and West Virginia. His band was called the Blue Grass Boys. By 1950, it was famous across America. The band gave its name to the music it played—bluegrass.

3 A bluegrass band may be led by a mandolin, banjo, or fiddle player. Most bands have all three instruments. Usually, there are a guitar and a bass as well.

4 Bluegrass festivals take place all over the country throughout the summer. Most of them are held in small country towns. People come from all over to hear the music. The Appalachians are still the home of bluegrass. But fans—and bands—come from as far away as Mexico, England, and Japan. The fans bring their own instruments. They make their own music between sets by the stars. They trade tapes. The stars mix with the fans and give them lessons.

5 Bill Monroe was once hailed by President Ronald Reagan as "the only living American who created a style of music." Monroe died in 1996. But young musicians today are still learning bluegrass and sharing the music with the people.

Circle the correct answer for questions 1–5.
Write your answer to question 6 on a separate piece of paper.

1. Bluegrass is a form of ______.
   - **A** jazz
   - **B** salsa music
   - **C** rock and roll
   - **D** country music

2. Which word in paragraph 5 means "honored, or saluted"?
   - **A** died
   - **B** style
   - **C** hailed
   - **D** created

3. Which paragraph tells about bluegrass fans?
   - **A** 1
   - **B** 2
   - **C** 3
   - **D** 4

4. What happened last in the article?
   - **A** Bill Monroe played with the Blue Grass Boys.
   - **B** Bill Monroe was hailed by President Reagan.
   - **C** Bill Monroe's band named its music.
   - **D** Bill Monroe became a star.

5. You can decide from the article that bluegrass ______.
   - **A** sounds like rock and roll
   - **B** is popular only in Kentucky
   - **C** is still a popular form of music
   - **D** needs a large band to play it

6. Who is a musical hero to you? Describe what he or she does and tell why this person is your hero.

What are puffballs?

1 Puffballs are mushrooms that don't follow the rules. They have no caps, stems, or other usual mushroom parts. In fact, you never see the whole puffball. You see only its fruit. It's like looking at an apple without ever seeing the tree.

2 Puffballs grow in rich, moist soil. Underground, they have a network of white threads. When the temperature is just right, little bumps develop on the tangled threads. The bumps swell up like balloons and push through the soil. These are the puffballs you see. Some will be two or three inches wide, while others grow to be six feet around.

3 At first, each puffball is firm and white. Slowly the inside part gets soft and brown. It is filled with threads and with spores, the seeds of the puffball. Spores are so tiny that they can't be seen without a microscope. One puffball can hold ten trillion of them.

4 As the inside of the puffball matures, the outside covering dries out. Cracks appear in it. If you tap the puffball now, it explodes. A cloud of spores flies out. A few dry threads and some bits of the outer covering are all that remain of the puffball. The spores are carried away by the wind. Only one in a trillion lands on rich, moist soil. That spore divides and divides again. Soon it grows into a new network of underground threads. More puffballs are on the way.

Circle the correct answer for questions 1–5.
Write your answer to question 6 on a separate piece of paper.

1. The article does *not* tell about the ______ of a puffball.
   - **A** smell
   - **B** spores
   - **C** color
   - **D** size

2. Which word in paragraph 4 means "reaches full growth"?
   - **A** dries
   - **B** divides
   - **C** explodes
   - **D** matures

3. Which paragraph tells how puffballs look different from other mushrooms?
   - **A** 1
   - **B** 2
   - **C** 3
   - **D** 4

4. What does *not* happen to the white threads of the puffball?
   - **A** Bumps turn black.
   - **B** Bumps develop on them.
   - **C** Bumps swell up like balloons.
   - **D** Bumps push through the soil.

5. *Swell* can have the following meanings. Mark the meaning used in paragraph 2.
   - **A** great
   - **B** fill with pride
   - **C** slow ocean wave
   - **D** grow bigger due to inside pressure

6. Puffballs can be eaten, but only at a certain stage of their growth. When do you think that would be, and why? Can you think of any other plants or flowers that can be eaten? How are they like the puffball? How are they different?

Who is I. M. Pei?

1 You are looking up at the John Hancock Tower in Boston. The skyscraper is covered in blue-green glass. Reflected in the glass are the 200-year-old buildings of Copley Square below. Now you're in Cleveland. Inside the Rock and Roll Hall of Fame is a stunning pyramid of glass. It is upside down and seems to lean against the building's solid mass. Here is another glass pyramid. It stands outside the Louvre, a famous art museum in Paris, France. It looks as old as Egypt, yet as new as today.

2 All these buildings were designed by one architect: I. M. Pei. So were many other buildings around the world. They include museums and office towers, laboratories and libraries. Pei has built hotels, concert halls, convention centers, and housing for poor people.

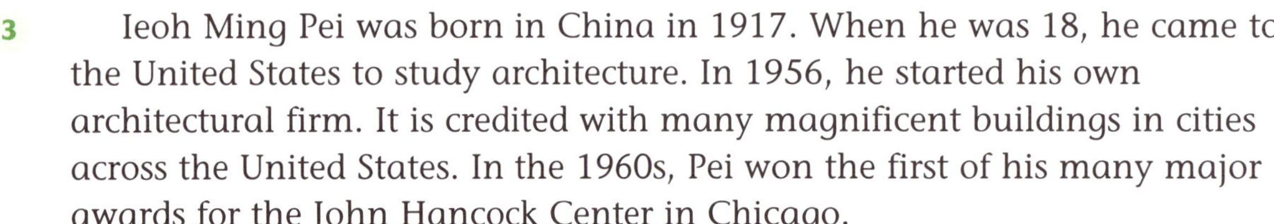

3 Ieoh Ming Pei was born in China in 1917. When he was 18, he came to the United States to study architecture. In 1956, he started his own architectural firm. It is credited with many magnificent buildings in cities across the United States. In the 1960s, Pei won the first of his many major awards for the John Hancock Center in Chicago.

4 An I. M. Pei building is a work of art. It has clean, sharp lines. It blends with the surrounding space in pleasing ways. It combines glass with striking forms to fill spaces with light. Yet a Pei building is designed for use. Architecture, Pei said, becomes art only when it is "built on a foundation of need."

Circle the correct answer for questions 1–5.
Write your answer to question 6 on a separate piece of paper.

1. The Rock and Roll Hall of Fame is in ______.
   - A Boston
   - B Chicago
   - C Cleveland
   - D Los Angeles

2. Which word in paragraph 4 means "a base that supports something"?
   - A architecture
   - B foundation
   - C building
   - D space

3. Which paragraph tells what makes an I. M. Pei building special?
   - A 1
   - B 2
   - C 3
   - D 4

4. You can decide from the article that I. M. Pei ______.
   - A works only in the United States
   - B started a very successful business
   - C prefers old-fashioned buildings
   - D designs all his buildings the same

5. *Striking* can have the following meanings. Mark the meaning used in paragraph 4.
   - A attention-getting
   - B stopping work
   - C discovering
   - D hitting

6. What building would you consider a work of art? Explain why.

What is an ani?

1 The word *ani* (ah•NEE) sounds like a name someone made up. But there really is an ani. It is a shiny black bird that lives in South and Central America. Its arched beak is almost as high as it is long. That's not what makes this bird different, though. Anis raise their young in an unusual way.

2 The anis share every part of their daily life. During the day, the birds fly very close together. They follow every turn of their leader. Now and then they rest—in the same place, of course. And when the sun goes down, the friendly flock roosts together, huddled side by side in a favorite bush.

3 Many other birds live together this way—for a while. When the time comes to raise their families, they go their separate ways. Not the anis. Every bird in the flock helps to build one large community nest. It is a rather shaggy arrangement of twigs stuck in a bush. All the females, as many as 20, lay their eggs in this same nest. Then all the anis, male and female, share the duties of hatching the eggs and caring for the chicks.

4 The ani is related to the cuckoo bird. This may seem strange, because the European cuckoo is known for being lazy. The mother cuckoo bird lays her eggs in the nests of other birds and lets them raise her chicks. With their expert child care, the anis do more than their share to improve the image of the cuckoo family.

Circle the correct answer for questions 1–5.
Write your answer to question 6 on a separate piece of paper.

1. The article does *not* tell about the ______ of the ani.
   - **A** nest
   - **B** flock
   - **C** food
   - **D** looks

2. Which word in paragraph 3 means "the way or style in which things are put together"?
   - **A** bush
   - **B** flock
   - **C** community
   - **D** arrangement

3. Which paragraph compares the ani to the cuckoo?
   - **A** 1
   - **B** 2
   - **C** 3
   - **D** 4

4. What does *not* happen before an ani is born?
   - **A** The males leave the nest.
   - **B** The flock builds a community nest.
   - **C** The females lay their eggs in the same nest.
   - **D** The males and females help hatch the eggs.

5. You can conclude from the article that anis ______.
   - **A** go their separate ways after the eggs hatch
   - **B** care for chicks other than their own
   - **C** don't live in large groups
   - **D** are a lot like the cuckoo

6. Why do you think the anis live as they do? Can you think of anything that people do that is similar to the anis' way of life?

Who was "The Yellow Kid"?

1 Joseph Pulitzer was always looking for new ways to make money. He was the publisher of the New York *World* and other newspapers. On his staff was an artist named Richard Outcault. In 1895, Pulitzer had Outcault start drawing a weekly cartoon. It appeared in the Sunday edition of the *World.* Pulitzer hoped it would make more people read his paper.

2 The cartoon was titled "Down Hogan's Alley." It featured a grinning, wisecracking little boy. He was bald. His ears stuck out. He was always barefoot and dressed in a nightshirt. The words he "spoke" were written on his clothes. The boy had no name. But soon after he first appeared, Pulitzer began experimenting with colored printing inks. The boy's nightshirt was printed in yellow. People called him "The Yellow Kid."

3 The cartoon was successful, so Outcault asked his boss for a raise. When Pulitzer refused, Outcault quit. He went to work for another newspaper, the *Journal American.* Pulitzer hired another cartoonist to draw the Yellow Kid. Soon the cartoon was appearing in both papers.

4 Other cartoons followed. "The Katzenjammer Kids" appeared in 1897. Its artist, Rudolph Dirks, came up with some new ideas. He used a strip, or series, of cartoons to tell a story. He wrote characters' words not on their clothes but in "balloons" above their heads. By 1910, hundreds of "comic strips" were appearing in newspapers across the United States.

5 Stories told in cartoons go back to the ancient Egyptians. But "The Yellow Kid" is considered part of the first modern newspaper comic.

Circle the correct answer for questions 1–5.
Write your answer to question 6 on a separate piece of paper.

1. The first newspaper cartoon was titled ______.
   - **A** "The Katzenjammer Kids"
   - **B** "Down Hogan's Alley"
   - **C** "Richard Outcault"
   - **D** "The Yellow Kid"

2. Which word in paragraph 2 means "making clever, funny remarks"?
   - **A** printing
   - **B** grinning
   - **C** wisecracking
   - **D** experimenting

3. Which paragraph tells how cartoon balloons came about?
   - **A** 1
   - **B** 2
   - **C** 3
   - **D** 4

4. What happened first in the article?
   - **A** Outcault asked for a raise.
   - **B** Pulitzer hired another cartoonist.
   - **C** Outcault began drawing a weekly cartoon.
   - **D** Pulitzer experimented with colored printing inks.

5. You can decide from the article that comic strips ______.
   - **A** became popular across the United States
   - **B** became less popular after 1910
   - **C** usually don't tell a story
   - **D** are easy to draw

6. Imagine that you are the main character in your favorite newspaper comic. Write a short story about your adventures.

How does a snake move?

1 Few animals in motion are more graceful than a snake. Different kinds of snakes may travel in different ways. But each moves with ease and grace. Many snakes swim as well as they glide on land. Some are skillful tree climbers. And all this is done without hands or feet, arms or legs.

2 A snake travels by bending its body in waves from side to side. It can make this wavy motion because of its flexible spine, its many ribs, and its smooth ribbons of muscle. A long snake may have 300 to 400 pairs of ribs. Each rib is attached to the snake's spine. The ribs curve around, making a tubelike cage for the snake's body. When the snake makes a U-turn, the ribs on the inside of the turn gather together. Those on the outside spread apart. As the snake glides along, the spreading and closing ribs switch from side to side in a rippling motion.

3 At this point, the snake might go backward or forward. What keeps it moving ahead are special scales on its underside. These scales are larger and stiffer than the snake's other scales. They keep it from sliding backward. The snake also makes use of stones, grassy spots, and other bumps on the ground to keep itself moving forward. That is why a snake cannot move easily across a sheet of glass. The important thing, if you happen to be a snake, is to get a good hold on a surface. The rest will take care of itself.

Circle the correct answer for questions 1–5.
Write your answer to question 6 on a separate piece of paper.

1. A snake does *not* use ______ to move.
   - **A** ribs
   - **B** legs
   - **C** scales
   - **D** muscles

2. Which word in paragraph 2 means "easy to bend or twist"?
   - **A** smooth
   - **B** flexible
   - **C** rippling
   - **D** spreading

3. ______ keep a snake moving ahead.
   - **A** Smooth surfaces
   - **B** Scales on its underside
   - **C** Spreading and closing ribs
   - **D** Smooth ribbons of muscle

4. You can decide from the article that a snake would have the most trouble moving forward on a ______.
   - **A** mirror
   - **B** beach
   - **C** tree
   - **D** rug

5. *Scales* have the following meanings. Mark the meaning used in paragraph 3.
   - **A** climbs
   - **B** regulates up or down
   - **C** machines for weighing
   - **D** body covering of an animal

6. Many people are afraid of all kinds of snakes. Are you? Tell why or why not.

Who was Otzi the Iceman?

1 While hiking in the Italian Alps on September 19, 1991, Erika and Helmut Simon discovered the frozen body of a man. At first they thought it was the body of a modern hiker. When the body was removed from the ice, scientists were surprised to find out that the body was more than 5,000 years old. The mummy became known as Otzi the Iceman.

2 By studying Otzi, scientists have learned valuable information about the way ancient people lived. Otzi was wearing leather shoes lined with straw, clothing made of leather and plant fibers, and a fur coat and hat. He was carrying a wooden backpack and several tools. The tools included a copper ax, a stone knife, a bow and arrow, and an arrow repair kit.

3 At the time of his death, Otzi was between 30 and 45 years old. He was about 5′3″ tall. Based on his clothes and tools, scientists believe he was a hunter. The snow and ice and surrounding rocks in the place where he died helped preserve his body.

4 Otzi is now kept at the South Tyrol Museum of Archaeology in Bolzano, Italy. If you ever have the chance to visit, bring your coat. Otzi's body is kept at 21°F in order to preserve it. As scientists develop more tests and better technology, they hope to keep studying Otzi in order to learn more about our early ancestors.

Circle the correct answer for questions 1–5.
Write your answer to question 6 on a separate piece of paper.

1. The article does *not* tell ______.
   - **A** how Otzi died
   - **B** who found Otzi
   - **C** what Otzi was wearing
   - **D** what tools Otzi was carrying

2. Which word in paragraph 2 means "very old"?
   - **A** wooden
   - **B** several
   - **C** valuable
   - **D** ancient

3. Which paragraph tells why scientists think Otzi was a hunter?
   - **A** 1
   - **B** 2
   - **C** 3
   - **D** 4

4. If you visit Otzi, you should bring a coat because ______.
   - **A** Otzi was a hunter
   - **B** Otzi was also wearing one
   - **C** Otzi's body is kept in the mountains
   - **D** Otzi's body is kept at a cold temperature

5. You can decide from the article that ______.
   - **A** Otzi did not know how to make clothes and tools
   - **B** Otzi was the leader of his people
   - **C** Otzi lived in a cold climate
   - **D** Otzi had a large family

6. Compare the clothes Otzi wore to the clothes you wear in winter. How are they alike? How are they different?

What was a quagga?

1 The quagga has been described as an unfinished zebra. This animal was about the size of a small horse. Its body was light brown, with stripes only on the head, neck, and front part. A dark brown line ran down the middle of its back. Its ears and tail were like a donkey's. Its legs were white with black hoofs. The quagga made a strange noise that sounded like "KWA-guh." It got its name from this barking neigh.

2 The story of the quagga is a sad one. Herds of the wild animals once ran free over the plains of South Africa. When they rushed by, the noise was compared to a great storm. Then settlers from Europe came to South Africa in the 1600s. Although they didn't like the taste of quagga meat, their workers did. Quaggas were easy to hunt, and the meat cost no money. Their hides were also useful for making sacks and shoes. The settlers killed quaggas by the hundreds. No one seemed to realize that the animals were dying out.

3 Quaggas were easy to tame. It would have been simple to raise them for meat and skins the way cattle are raised. But no one thought of that. People continued to hunt and kill the quaggas. Finally, in 1873, there was only one quagga alive in the entire world—a female living in a zoo in the Netherlands. The lone quagga died in 1883.

Circle the correct answer for questions 1–5.
Write your answer to question 6 on a separate piece of paper.

1. The article does *not* tell about the ______ of the quagga.
   - A neigh
   - B food
   - C hoofs
   - D size

2. Which word in paragraph 2 means "groups of animals that live or are kept together"?
   - A sacks
   - B herds
   - C settlers
   - D hides

3. What is the main idea of the article?
   - A The quagga was a unique animal that was killed off by settlers.
   - B The quagga once ran free over the plains of South Africa.
   - C The quagga was easy to hunt and tame.
   - D The quagga looked similar to the zebra.

4. The quagga died off because ______.
   - A it was taken to zoos
   - B it was part dinosaur
   - C it was killed by the hundreds
   - D it was raised for meat and skins

5. You can decide from the article that the quagga was called an unfinished zebra because it ______.
   - A died out
   - B lived in South Africa
   - C was like a small horse
   - D was not striped all over

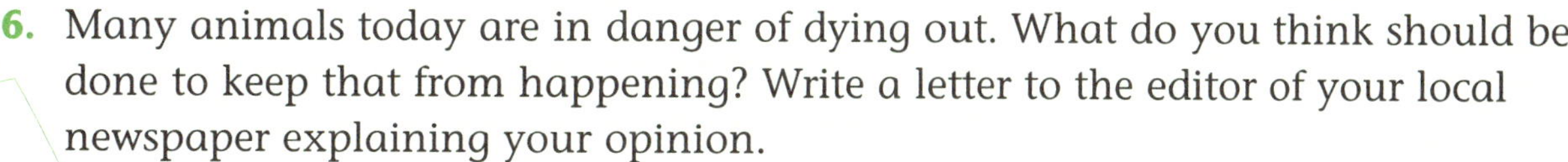

6. Many animals today are in danger of dying out. What do you think should be done to keep that from happening? Write a letter to the editor of your local newspaper explaining your opinion.

How did dogs save Nome, Alaska?

1 In January 1925, the town of Nome, Alaska, faced a deadly threat. A dangerous sickness called diphtheria was spreading through the town. Some people had already died. Many more would die without medicine. The only thing that could stop the spread of the disease was a medicine that was nearly 900 miles away in Anchorage.

2 Unfortunately, getting the medicine to Nome would not be easy. The weather was so bad that airplanes and trains could not get all the way there. The only way to get the medicine to Nome was by dogsled. A train took the medicine the first 220 miles. From there, teams of sled dogs would have to take the medicine the 674 miles to Nome.

3 More than 20 people—called "mushers"—and sled dog teams took part in the relay. They traveled through temperatures that were almost 40° below zero. Many times, the wind was strong enough to knock over sleds and dogs. The snowy conditions often made it difficult to stay on course.

4 On February 2, 1925, six days after the journey began, Gunnar Kaassen and his team of sled dogs arrived in Nome with the medicine. They were cold and exhausted. Kaassen said it was the most difficult trip he had ever made. Today, a famous dogsled race called the Iditarod helps us remember the life-saving efforts of these brave men and dogs.

Circle the correct answer for questions 1–5.
Write your answer to question 6 on a separate piece of paper.

1. The deadly threat facing Nome, Alaska, was ______.
   - **A** freezing temperatures
   - **B** snowy conditions
   - **C** strong winds
   - **D** a sickness

2. Which word in paragraph 4 means "very tired"?
   - **A** exhausted
   - **B** difficult
   - **C** brave
   - **D** cold

3. Which paragraph describes the mushers' journey?
   - **A** 1
   - **B** 2
   - **C** 3
   - **D** 4

4. You can decide from the article that if the dog teams had not been successful ______.
   - **A** many people would have died
   - **B** a train or airplane would have had to take over
   - **C** the town of Nome would have been covered in snow
   - **D** the people in the town would have gotten better on their own

5. *Course* can have the following meanings. Mark the meaning used in paragraph 3.
   - **A** a class
   - **B** a path
   - **C** a plan of action
   - **D** an area where a competition is held

6. Imagine that you lived in Nome, Alaska, in 1925. Write a paragraph about how you felt when you heard that the medicine had arrived.

How are porcupines born and raised?

1 When a porcupine is born, it looks like a living pincushion. It has thousands of quills partly hidden in its thick, dark fur. Many people think that its birth must be hard for its mother. However, it isn't a problem at all. The baby is born inside a membrane something like a tough plastic bag. Its whole body—fur and quills—is damp. The quills are soft, and they bend easily. They do not harden into sharp little needles until the air dries them.

2 A quill is really a kind of stiff hair that is loosely attached to the porcupine's skin at one end. It is the porcupine's protection. Sometimes the outside end of the quill is turned back into a sharp hook. The hook sticks into anything that hits it. Then the quill pulls loose from the porcupine's skin. The porcupine does not "throw" it as some people believe.

3 A newborn porcupine is about as big as a fist and weighs about a pound. The young animal feeds on its mother's milk for the first month or so. The two are able to live side by side because they keep their quills relaxed and flat. They do not want to hurt each other. After the baby is six months old, it hardly ever sees its mother. The porcupine learns to eat leaves and twigs and is able to survive on its own.

Circle the correct answer for questions 1–5.
Write your answer to question 6 on a separate piece of paper.

1. When a porcupine is born, its quills are ______.
   - **A** like needles
   - **B** tough
   - **C** soft
   - **D** dry

2. Which word in paragraph 1 means "slightly wet"?
   - **A** damp
   - **B** dark
   - **C** tough
   - **D** thick

3. What happens last in the life of a baby porcupine?
   - **A** It feeds on its mother's milk.
   - **B** It separates from its mother.
   - **C** Its fur dries for the first time.
   - **D** It lives side by side with its mother.

4. You can decide from the article that ______.
   - **A** porcupines don't need their quills
   - **B** most porcupines like to attack people
   - **C** a baby porcupine doesn't need its mother
   - **D** it is painful to brush against an adult porcupine

5. *Leaves* can have the following meanings. Mark the meaning used in paragraph 3.
   - **A** quits
   - **B** goes away
   - **C** fails to include
   - **D** parts of plants and trees

6. Animals sometimes die after a run-in with a porcupine. Why do you think this is so?

What did Thor Heyerdahl prove?

1 How far would you go to solve a mystery? Thor Heyerdahl (HY•ur•dahl), a scientist and writer from Norway, once traveled more than 4,000 miles to attempt to explain one.

2 Years ago, explorers found people living on the South Sea Islands of the Pacific Ocean. The people had fine farms and villages. They had also built temples and made tall stone statues. But where had the people come from? How had they gotten to these islands in the middle of the world's largest ocean?

3 Thor Heyerdahl thought that he knew the answer. The Indians of Peru in South America had also built tall stone statues, temples, and large villages. Thor believed that hundreds of years ago these Indians had sailed to the South Sea Islands on rafts. Most other scientists did not agree with him. "Impossible!" they said. "Imagine sailing 4,300 miles on an open raft! It just couldn't be done."

4 Thor decided to test his theory. He built a raft just like the ones used by the Indians of Peru. Then on April 28, 1947, he and five friends set out from Peru for the South Seas. On board the *Kon-Tiki,* the men battled hot sun, huge waves, and killer sharks. Finally, after 101 days, they reached the South Sea Islands. Their daring voyage showed that Thor Heyerdahl may have been right. The ancient Indians of Peru could have sailed to those distant islands.

Circle the correct answer for questions 1–5.
Write your answer to question 6 on a separate piece of paper.

1. The article does *not* tell how Thor Heyerdahl ______.
   - **A** fought ocean pollution
   - **B** made a sea voyage
   - **C** tested a theory
   - **D** built a raft

2. Which word in paragraph 1 means "to try"?
   - **A** go
   - **B** solve
   - **C** explain
   - **D** attempt

3. Which paragraph tells why Thor thought the people of the South Sea Islands might be from Peru?
   - **A** 1
   - **B** 2
   - **C** 3
   - **D** 4

4. Which event happened first in history?
   - **A** People settled on the South Sea Islands.
   - **B** The *Kon-Tiki* reached the South Sea Islands.
   - **C** Thor Heyerdahl left Peru on the *Kon-Tiki*.
   - **D** Thor Heyerdahl traveled from Norway to Peru.

5. You can conclude from the article that scientists ______.
   - **A** enjoy sailing
   - **B** are not always right
   - **C** dislike Thor Heyerdahl
   - **D** know a lot about the South Sea Islands

6. Write directions for making a raft. Be sure to explain the materials needed and the steps a person would go through.

How tough are badgers?

1 If you were asked to name a strong animal, you might think of a lion, an elephant, or even a bear. But would you think of a badger? After all, it's only 2 to 3 feet long and 8 to 25 pounds. Actually, though, scientists have found that for its size, the badger is one of the strongest and toughest animals around.

2 Badgers have many natural skills. One of them is digging. Badgers have long claws and webbed paws. They can scoop up lots of dirt easily and quickly. They make underground tunnels where they raise their young. They can also use these burrows to escape from an enemy.

3 But badgers don't have many enemies and seldom get into real trouble. That's because they are good fighters. Badgers are members of the weasel family. Like their cousins the wolverines, badgers can be very mean when they are threatened. Badgers have sharp fangs and very loose skin. If a coyote, dog, or mountain lion grabs a badger by its fur, the animal can spin right around and bite back.

4 Badgers defend themselves in another way as well. Their faces are striped with black and white markings. When an animal comes too close to a badger's back, it turns and points its face at the animal. It may growl and hiss, too. This will usually scare the animal away. In fact, those markings are how the badger got its name. Its face is like a bright badge that it wears proudly.

5 And why not? While the badger never looks for a fight, this tough little animal certainly knows how to take care of itself.

Circle the correct answer for questions 1–5.
Write your answer to question 6 on a separate piece of paper.

1. The badger is a member of the ______ family.
   - **A** bear
   - **B** weasel
   - **C** raccoon
   - **D** prairie dog

2. Which word in paragraph 3 means "in danger"?
   - **A** seldom
   - **B** mean
   - **C** sharp
   - **D** threatened

3. Which paragraph tells where badgers raise their young?
   - **A** 1
   - **B** 2
   - **C** 3
   - **D** 4

4. If an animal grabs a badger by its fur, what is the badger likely to do?
   - **A** It will play dead.
   - **B** It will escape and run up a tree.
   - **C** It will spin around and bite back.
   - **D** It will change the color of its face.

5. *Scoop* can have the following meanings. Mark the meaning used in paragraph 2.
   - **A** dig out
   - **B** hot tip on a news story
   - **C** deep spoon for ice cream
   - **D** neckline on a woman's dress

6. Do you think a badger would make a good pet? Why or why not?

Where do new words come from?

1 New words can come from almost anywhere. Did you know that a favorite toy was named for one of our strongest presidents? Theodore Roosevelt, known as Teddy, once saved a small bear from being shot. When the story was told, toymakers began making stuffed toy bears. The new toy was called "teddy bear," of course.

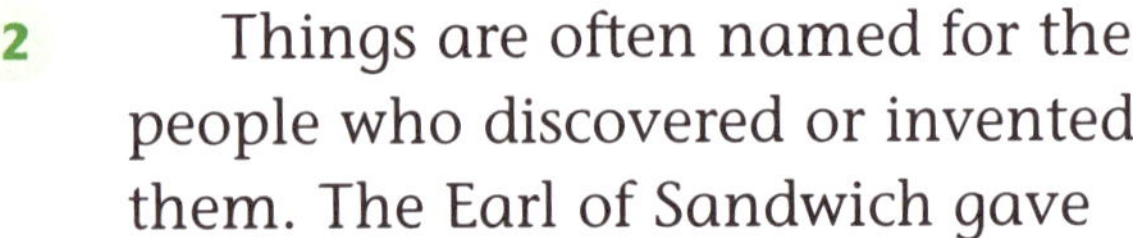

2 Things are often named for the people who discovered or invented them. The Earl of Sandwich gave his name to a new way to eat food, the sandwich. Anders Dahl had a flower named after him—the dahlia. The watt, a measurement of electricity, was named after a pioneer in the field, James Watt. Hundreds of words have come about this way.

3 Many of our words are simply borrowed from other languages. The word *pizza* is Italian. *Banjo* is African. *Chipmunk* is Native American. *Rodeo* is Spanish, and so on. Other new words are made by putting old words together. Because of computers, words like *website, software,* and *chatroom* have been formed this way. Sometimes two words blend together to make a new word, like *smog* from *smoke* and *fog.* Still other words are made up by fitting a sound to a meaning. *Whoosh* and *vroom* are words of this kind.

4 The English language now has over one million words. Thousands more are added each year. People are always working on ways to make our world better. And new inventions, ideas, and discoveries need new words to tell about them.

Circle the correct answer for questions 1–5.
Write your answer to question 6 on a separate piece of paper.

1. The article does *not* tell about new words coming from ______.

   A abbreviations or initials
   B other languages
   C people's names
   D sounds

2. Which word in paragraph 2 means "one of the first to do something"?

   A dahlia
   B field
   C watt
   D pioneer

3. Which paragraph tells how the word *vroom* was made up?

   A 1
   B 2
   C 3
   D 4

4. What is the main idea of the article?

   A New words are created constantly and can come from almost anywhere.
   B Things are often named for people who discover them.
   C New inventions need new words to tell about them.
   D Many words are borrowed from other languages.

5. You can conclude from the article that dictionaries ______.

   A are printed in only one language
   B are rewritten each year
   C must be changed often
   D aren't very helpful

6. Create a new word of your own and write a letter to the editor of a dictionary to persuade him or her that the word is important and that it should be added to the next edition of the dictionary.

What do hurricane hunters do?

1 When a hurricane is approaching, most people try to get away from it in order to stay safe. However, a few brave men and women fly airplanes directly into the center of the storm. These "hurricane hunters" give scientists and weather forecasters valuable information about the strength of the storm and how fast it is growing.

2 Even though weather satellites can warn forecasters that a hurricane is approaching, that is not the most accurate way to measure the strength of the storm. In fact, satellite estimates of a storm's strength can be off by as much as a category. That means that what seems to be a serious Category 2 storm could actually be a very dangerous Category 3 storm. By flying into the storm, hurricane hunters can use special instruments to gather better information.

3 When hurricane hunters enter the storm, they release instruments that measure temperature, air pressure, wind speed, and wind direction. Each mission lasts about ten hours. The crew passes through the storm between four and six times to collect the most detailed information.

4 After the hurricane hunters have collected all the information, they give it to the forecasters at the National Hurricane Center. The scientists there use the information to determine if and when a hurricane is going to approach a coastline and come on land. This allows them to decide what kind of action to take to warn people and keep them safe.

Circle the correct answer for questions 1–5.
Write your answer to question 6 on a separate piece of paper.

1. Hurricane hunters fly ______.
   - **A** over hurricanes
   - **B** under hurricanes
   - **C** into hurricanes
   - **D** around hurricanes

2. Which word in paragraph 3 means "let go of"?
   - **A** release
   - **B** measure
   - **C** collect
   - **D** enter

3. Which paragraph tells how hurricane hunters collect information about a hurricane?
   - **A** 1
   - **B** 2
   - **C** 3
   - **D** 4

4. After hurricane hunters collect information, they ______.
   - **A** decide what kind of action to take
   - **B** release special instruments
   - **C** pass through the storm
   - **D** give it to forecasters

5. You can conclude from the article that ______.
   - **A** the measurements from hurricane hunters are more accurate than satellite measurements
   - **B** satellite measurements are more accurate than the measurements from hurricane hunters
   - **C** satellite measurements and measurements from hurricane hunters are equally accurate
   - **D** neither hurricane hunters nor satellites provide accurate measurements

6. Would you like to be a hurricane hunter? Explain why or why not.

What is Death Valley?

1 The lowest piece of land in the Western Hemisphere is a desert valley that stretches across parts of California and Nevada. It is 282 feet below sea level in places. This valley is also very hot. In summer, afternoon temperatures often reach 120°F. Once the temperature hit a sizzling 134°F. The name of this area is Death Valley.

2 Death Valley got its name in 1850. Some settlers were coming west to look for gold. Because of a mistake on their map, they got lost. One of the men found a way out of the desert valley and got help for the others. Leaving at last, a woman looked back and said, "Good-bye, Death Valley." The name stuck.

3 In spite of its name, Death Valley is full of life. Burros, birds, snakes, lizards, and rare bighorn sheep live there. So do some unusual fish called pupfish. They may be Death Valley's oldest living animals. The tiny pupfish have lived in the valley's streams and pools for thousands of years.

4 Death Valley also has many human visitors. In 1933, it was made a national monument. Its 3,000 square miles were set apart for people's enjoyment. Each year more than half a million tourists come to the valley. They appreciate its beautiful scenery as well as its camping grounds, museum, and deserted mining towns. Despite the heat, Death Valley is a popular landmark.

Circle the correct answer for questions 1–5.
Write your answer to question 6 on a separate piece of paper.

1. The article does *not* tell about the ______ of Death Valley.
   - **A** animals
   - **B** plants
   - **C** heat
   - **D** visitors

2. Which word in paragraph 4 means "pleasure"?
   - **A** museum
   - **B** scenery
   - **C** enjoyment
   - **D** monument

3. Which paragraph tells how Death Valley got its name?
   - **A** 1
   - **B** 2
   - **C** 3
   - **D** 4

4. Death Valley got its name when ______.
   - **A** settlers got lost there
   - **B** Nevada was named a state
   - **C** dead animals were found there
   - **D** it was made a national monument

5. You can decide from the article that Death Valley ______.
   - **A** has a volcano
   - **B** gets a lot of rain
   - **C** is an unusual place
   - **D** is comfortable in the summer

6. Imagine that you are a settler who gets lost in Death Valley. Write a story that includes details on how you feel, what you see, and how you plan to get out.

What are "smart" buildings?

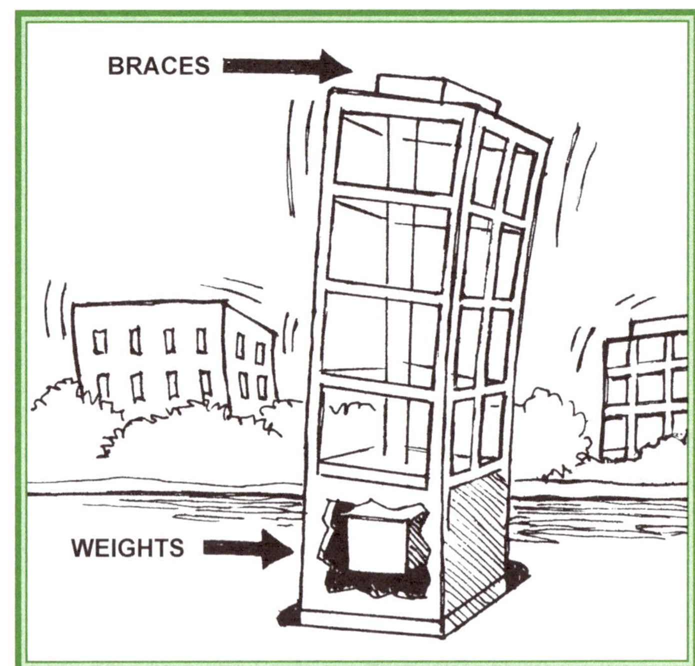

1 Have you ever seen a movie of a city being hit by an earthquake? The ground splits open, everything shakes, and tall buildings topple. Unfortunately, this can happen in real life, especially in places where buildings have been built in old-fashioned ways.

2 But now scientists and engineers are finding better ways to build skyscrapers. These buildings can keep standing even during a major earthquake. In fact, some "smart" buildings have been made so that they will hardly feel any shaking at all.

3 What makes these buildings so strong? Believe it or not, the answer is that they don't stand still during an earthquake. They actually *move*. They just move in the opposite way of each shake of the building.

4 There are three ways that these smart buildings do this. Some buildings have huge weights in them. These weights glide back and forth when the building shakes. They help the building to "balance" itself, just like a person does when trying to stand on one foot. Another way a smart building moves is through the use of strong metal ropes or braces. These pull the building back into its correct position if it starts to move off its center. A third way is for a smart building to use jets of water or air to push itself back into place.

5 All three ways are guided by special computers. These sense the slightest shaking and react in less than a second. Buildings are "smart" now because smart people are building them.

Circle the correct answer for questions 1–5.
Write your answer to question 6 on a separate piece of paper.

1. The article does *not* tell ______.
   - **A** how smart buildings are built
   - **B** why smart buildings don't fall
   - **C** why smart buildings have weights
   - **D** when the first smart buildings were built

2. Which word in paragraph 1 means "fall down"?
   - **A** hit
   - **B** splits
   - **C** topple
   - **D** happen

3. Which paragraph tells about the three ways smart buildings move in a big earthquake?
   - **A** 1
   - **B** 2
   - **C** 3
   - **D** 4

4. You can decide from the article that smart buildings are most popular ______.
   - **A** in old-fashioned neighborhoods
   - **B** in areas that have earthquakes
   - **C** in areas that have heavy rain
   - **D** in housing developments

5. *Major* can have the following meanings. Mark the meaning used in paragraph 2.
   - **A** greater in amount or importance
   - **B** very serious, as an illness
   - **C** an officer in the army
   - **D** main field of study

6. How do you think scientists and engineers test their ideas before they build new skyscrapers?